SmallBiz Checkup

*Grow Simply
Simply Grow*

Chris Mumford

Acknowledgements

I am thankful that Karen Kerrigan first suggested the idea of creating a small business checkup by using Joe Startup. Phil Dixon made the convincing pitch to make the book happen. I am grateful to Ken Yancey and Lou Davenport for testing the content. I would like to thank Michael McNabb and Vivek Kapur for their wonderful insights over the years. Matthew Estes has been my greatest mentor.

Special thanks to the artist Hannah Lewis-Marlow for her delightful drawings. I'm grateful to Clarissa Esguerra for her super design efforts. Thanks to William Murphy for his great editing.

Thanks to my wife, Joelle, and my kids, Eli and Alexi, and my parents, Stephen and Judy. You were in my thoughts when I wrote the book.

Copyright 2014 by Chris Mumford

All rights reserved. No part of this book shall be reproduced, stored in a retrieval system or transmitted by any means, electronic, mechanical, photocopying, recording or otherwise, without written permission of the publisher/author. Request to the author should be addressed to joe@joestartup.com.

Limit of Liability/disclaimer of Warranty: While the publisher and author have used their best efforts in preparing this book, they make no representations or warranties with respect to the accuracy or completeness of the contents of this book and specifically disclaim any implied warranties of merchantability or fitness for a particular purpose. The advice and strategies contained herein may not be suitable for your situation. You should consult with a professional where appropriate. Neither the publisher nor author shall be liable for any loss of profit or any other commercial damages, including but not limited to special, incidental, consequential, or other damages.

Library of Congress Cataloging-in-Publication Data: Pending

TABLE OF CONTENTS

FORWARD   p.1

INTRODUCTION   p.2

THINK

Customer Experience
p.3

Customer Path
p.6

Value Chain
p.10

Teamwork
p.17

Enterprise Haiku
p.21

Presentation
p.25

CREATE

Creative Mindset
p.31

Innovation Process
p.37

Product Haiku
p.42

Develop
p.46

Make
p.49

Process Map
p.55

TELL

Customer Profile
p.59

Positioning
p.63

Always Be Different
p.67

Message
p.71

Materials
p.75

Story
p.80

RUN

Right People
p.84

Leadership
p.89

Sales Cycle
p.92

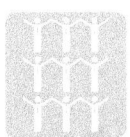
Sales Force
p.98

Budget
p.101

Fund Raising
p.105

FINAL THOUGHTS p.106

FORWARD

Many people believe that starting and running a small business is a daunting task fraught with peril, unknowns and unseen risks. For some it is like that, but it does not have to be. Taking the time to learn about starting and running a business, assessing skills gaps that you might have, doing a feasibility study and creating a plan that fills the gaps, addresses known risks and provides a path forward will make all the difference. It sounds like a huge undertaking but with the right support and the right tools it will not be.

Chris Mumford has used his considerable experience and research to write "SmallBiz Checkup" which breaks the business startup process down in to logical steps. There are easy-to-understand illustrations, examples and descriptions. The book and its lessons are also supported by the robust Joe Startup website that allows the entrepreneur to think, interact and create their own business concepts, as well as a plan to implement it. The opportunity to read, learn and absorb information in the book and then apply those lessons in an organized process at Joe Start up is a unique blend of learning tools that turn the information that you gathered into knowledge and a valuable output. It also simplifies the daunting task of starting or managing your business.

SCORE is an organization of more than 11,000 business men and women who volunteer their time and expertise to help small business owners and anyone wanting to start their own business. We have provided mentoring, coaching, counseling and training to over 10 million people since our inception in 1964. Our volunteers believe firmly in the value of creating and managing with a business plan. That plan should be based on an analysis of your business, identifying any strengths, weaknesses and gaps in your operations. Even if you did not start your business with a comprehensive business plan, it is not too late to create and use one. There are thousands of resources to help, including those at www.SCORE.org and now "SmallBiz Checkup" and the resources at "Joe Startup." Take the time, use the "SmallBiz Checkup" tools and resources, find a mentor, create a plan and be successful!

Good luck and good business,

Ken Yancey Jr.
CEO
SCORE

INTRODUCTION

The SmallBiz Checkup is written as an "un-business" business book where we minimize the business mumbo jumbo. The book is designed for time-crunched small business owners who want help finding solutions for their business gaps. The goal is to help owners look at their businesses with fresh eyes, seeing reality for what it is and realizing that they cannot be brilliant at all aspects of running a business. View your business as a startup, or a re-startup, by bringing new ideas to your business' most vexing problems.

Joe Startup is an easy-to-use biz-plan creator. We avoid the frumpy, traditional business plan format. The deliverable is an actionable biz-plan with clear tradeoffs formed by completing an objective, thorough examination of the business.

The book's content is not intended to be exhaustive, but distilled to the essentials. In other words, the content is the streetsmart advice an experienced mentor would give a small business owner.

The book is broken down into four processes: Think, Create, Tell, and Run. There are 24 step-by-step modules. Each lesson includes an introduction, examples, insights, instructions, and templates. Scan the QR codes to watch a video online or use online templates. While the lessons are designed to build on one another, the reader can jump around depending on learning preference.

This multimedia workbook is fully integrated with www.JoeStartup.com, a free, accompanying biz-plan creator which can be instantly shared with friends and advisors. Each reader can work at her own pace. The reader will have a plan to actually jumpstart his business upon completion of this book.

The inspiration for this book is that a simple-to-use biz-plan builder is needed to create an innovative, small-business revolution around the world. Joe Startup's creator, Chris Mumford, is a serial entrepreneur who has started businesses in the U.S. and Asia. He has served in the role of VP Sales and Marketing, VP Design, CFO, COO and CEO. He is on the faculty at the Kenan-Flagler business school at UNC Chapel Hill. The SmallBiz Checkup is a companion book to the Joe Startup Plan; startups and small businesses share 90% of the same DNA.

The ultimate goal of this book is simplicity. Writing a good biz-plan can be really, really hard, but learning how to write a plan need not be. Any Joe can do it.

If you choose to use the companion website:
1. Register on www.JoeStartup.com and set up a Google document, spreadsheet and presentation.
2. Edit your work in the book and transcribe to the Google templates.
3. Share your Joe Startup plan with friends and family on the website where they can provide real-time feedback in one place.

In the end, your online startup plan will include a two-minute intro video, presentation deck, budgets, charts, Text, and project plan.

Grow simply. Simply grow.

THINK

Customer Experience

Describe how your customer learns about and buys your product.

Watch Video
www.joestartup.com/module//think/customer-experience

Small business owners often have set views on who their customer is and what they want. However, customer types and needs can subtly shift over time. Other times, problem customers dominate much of the mindshare. Small business should objectively analyze their customer base a minimum of every six months. Look at the customer experience from a fresh perspective. Ask customers questions and collect data systematically.

Customer experience refers to the interaction of a customer with a product or a service. You can share stories of customer experience where you describe how customers first learn about your product and its key benefits, their experience in purchasing it, their expectations, and their experience or perception of the product's performance, including any product issues. These stories reveal key company processes and needed marketing materials.

1. Specifically describe the customers and their needs.

2. Explain how the customers first learn about your product. How do they research the products (online, in-store, or product-by-product comparison)? Answers to these questions will determine what marketing materials or strategies you need to explore.

3. How does your product solve their problem? What is the key benefit?

Responses to these should reflect your intended message to the customers.

4. How and where does the customer purchase the product? Data from these will show where the product should be sold.

5. What happens when the customer has a problem with the product? Information from this will help you develop processes to deal with product issues while maintaining a positive customer relationship. You will encounter product issues; being prepared is essential to converting an unhappy customer into a fiercely loyal customer.

The key point is to think about the business from the customer's perspective. Very often, business owners offer solutions from their perspectives only, often with negative outcomes. Regularly update your record of actual customer experience. Updated and accurate information will help your business adapt to real-world changing conditions.

 EXAMPLES

After having her first child, Margaret decided to move from New York City to her hometown in the mountains. The problem was that she didn't have a job. She had been the manager of a high-end housewares store in NYC but could not make motherhood, store managing, and maintaining an expensive apartment work. She would have to create her own job in the mountain tourist town. She wrote a customer experience story to help her start a business:

Our customer, moms, usually first learn about our store when they are window shopping on the main street. Their kids get ice cream or crepes, giving the mothers ample time to wander around the store for cool gifts and home goods. The store offers items that moms don't normally see at their hometown stores. Our product prices are higher, but that is okay; they are on vacation. If they have second thoughts and return a product, then we give them a free ice cream coupon. More than likely, the customer will find another interesting item to buy while their kids eat ice cream. In fact, we give free ice cream coupons, one per family, to the affluent lodges and hotels. This is a low-cost way to get target customers in our door.

Roy makes custom jewelry designed by kids for their mothers and grandmothers. Here is his consumer experience narrative:

Moms of home-schooled kids are always looking for projects for kids. These parents tend to use tightly knit social networks to share ideas. A mom reads about another mom raved over how her daughter sculpted some jewelers' wax, sent it to the jeweler, and received a fabulous sterling silver pendant. She gets compliments from her friends who also buy the product. Over time, the product crosses over into moms' discussions in general because it is so fun to talk about. The moms start posting pictures on Facebook, which gets more moms interested. Roy offers a 100% no-questions-asked return policy as few moms would return jewelry that their children made for them.

David was an average swimmer and an even worse lap counter. He started swimming late in life and often forgot how many laps he swam in an hour. So, he invented a simple lap counter that fit on his forefinger. Here is his customer experience narrative:

The customer first sees a swim lap counter in one of two ways. First, he notices other swimmers wearing a bright yellow ring on their forefinger. After seeing a few swimmers wearing the yellow ring, the customer asks about the ring. The customer can also learn about the product from a swim coach who might have been sent a free lap counter from the company. Triathletes will spend $40 for the lap counter as they already spend a lot on triathlon itself. If there is a problem, David sends a replacement immediately because he knows word of mouth is the best marketing method for his business.

? FAQ

What is the key benefit? The key benefit is the one element that the customer most values from the product. For example, most customers value their iPhone because it organizes their favorite music in one place. iPhones offer many benefits but, for many customers, music organization is the key benefit.

(i) INSTRUCTIONS

Overview: Tell the story of your customer learning about and buying the product

1. Describe the customer and their needs.

2. Explain how the customer first learns about the product/service.

3. Describe how the customer researches your product/service.

4. Explain the solutions your product offers.

5. Describe the key benefit.

6. Explain how and where the customer purchases the product.

7. Describe the customer interaction when there is a problem.

Customer Path
Understand how to sell your product to the customer.

Watch Video
www.joestartup.com/module//think/customer-path

A. Small business owners should often engage their customers to ask if there is a better way to provide a product/service, particularly when introducing a new offering. Over time, a small business will have to offer several ways for the customer to purchase the product. Business often spend their time perfecting products, giving little attention to determining the customer path. A customer path, or channel, refers to how a product or service gets to the customer.

For example, Apple's customer path includes retail sales through its stores, wholesale through cell phone stores like AT&T, and online sales.

B. The most common channels include retail sales, mail order catalog/online sales, direct sales, and wholesale. In retail store distribution, companies have their own sales outlets. Catalog/online sale is more straightforward.

Direct sales happen when company representatives directly call and sell to customers. Wholesale involves selling to another company, which then contacts or sells to another business or to the end customer.

THINK

Think through the customer path as soon as possible. Which customers can you sell to even before you've finished your product / service? Who can help you in sales? Start thinking how to sell your product while still developing it.

Here's an example: Milo, a pastry chef at a restaurant, wants to start a cake business. He makes fabulous cakes but does not know how to sell to customers.

Milo could wholesale to local shops. Or he could directly sell to his existing restaurant customers online.

Milo could also sell directly to his sister's customers who regularly have business parties. Each choice has its own benefits. Milo needs to make a decision.

Have a very clear idea of your customer path before you start your business.

 EXAMPLES

As a new mother, Joan currently has limited work opportunities. Joan has worked at the front counter of a meat shop in Montana since she was a teenager. The beef and bison jerky was a huge hit for the tourists. In fact, some tourists would call the store for follow up orders, but they could not take telephone orders. Joan had once approached the owners about starting a website but the owners weren't interested.

Joan was at a playdate when she saw Jennifer, an old friend who developed websites. By the end of the playdate, Joan decided she would develop a beef and bison jerky website. She could call on previous customers and promote the website through the retail store. After a couple of nervous days, the owners agreed to sell Joan the product at a wholesale price. Joan would be the "website agent," as long as they did not have to pay for the website. Joan was about to start the next chapter in her life.

Ted has developed a new line of scrubs for doctors and nurses. Although scrubs haven't changed in 50 years, textile technology has with wicking, antimicrobial and knit fabrics for greater comfort. Ted knew there were several channels to consider. The hospitals rented the cheapest scrubs from linen companies so that wasn't an option. Selling through retail stores was tough because Walmart and Scrubs and Beyond were forcing the mom-and-pop scrubs shops to close.

Ted looked into how to sell directly to doctors and nurses through tradeshows or online. Ted knew the old distribution channels were not the way to go, while the new channels could create opportunity, but at great risk.

Susan, a former pharmaceutical representative, had created a great sales award gift for high performing sales reps at large organizations. Her first customer was the sales vice president of her former company. They re-ordered quickly. After initial success, she called on sales award companies and several tradeshows. She had no success. When she was about to give up on the product, her friend Barbara asked how she sold the first order. Without thinking, Susan said that she called the assistant of the sales vice president to set up a meeting. Barbara suggested that she do the same for other companies and cut out the middlemen.

Susan found that getting CEOs and VPs to take meetings was nearly impossible but she could always get 5 minutes with their assistants. She found that if the assistants liked her product, then the assistants would immediately show their bosses and get results. After failing with the usual channels for months, she found that getting in the door and showing the first gatekeeper - the assistants - really paid off.

 FAQ

What is a customer path? A customer path is how you sell your product to the customer. This can be done directly, through stores, or through middlemen.

What is a channel? A channel is also a customer path.

What is the end customer? The end customer is the final buyer of the product. There are often middlemen, wholesalers or retailers who will buy and then resell to the final buyer.

What is direct sales? Direct sales is when a business sells directly to the end customer.

What is wholesale? Wholesale is when a business sells to another business who can sell to another business or the end customer.

What is retail stores? Retail store distribution is when a business sells to retail stores who sell to the end consumer.

What is mail order catalog/online sales? This type of sales is when the business sells directly to the end customer through its website or mail order catalog.

 INSTRUCTIONS

Overview: Understand how to sell your product to the customer

1. Decide which channels to sell your product through retail stores, mail order catalog/online sales, direct sales and wholesale.

_____

_____

2. Which customers can you sell to even before you've finished your product or service?

_____

_____

3. Who can help you in sales?

_____

_____

4. How can you get the sales pipeline going even before you finish your product?

_____

_____

Value Chain
Break your business down into simple parts.

Watch Video
www.joestartup.com/module//think/value-chain

Recently, my friend Josie told me that her business is experiencing growing pains. She felt overwhelmed by everything that needs to be done and was not sure where to start. Always start with a simple question, and then break the business down into blocks to make it easier to understand.

The simple question is: "Does the business create value?" Value, or profit, is selling a product or service for more than what it costs to make it. Profit means more money coming in than going out. If you sell a product for $5 and it costs you $2 to make, then that is a good business with a $3 profit.

A clear understanding of the chain helps identify the most valuable areas and gaps. You can determine if sales can grow through investing more money, or hiring someone in the valuable areas, or cutting costs by outsourcing the least valuable areas. In addition, you can estimate what changes can be made if you fill in the gaps. Most of all, this process will help create peace of mind in that you will understand the most valuable and underserved parts of your business. Now develop a plan to resolve those issues and create new opportunities.

1. Profit creation requires a whole chain of events. Break down a business into its four simplest processes: develop, make, tell, and sell. To develop is to invent a solution for a need. To make is to actually produce the product. To tell is to let customers know about the product and its benefits. To sell is to get customers to buy the product. Value is created if you can sell for more than it costs to make the product.

2. Use a value chain to understand the steps needed to start a business. You can focus on combining the most valuable chain links and on carrying out what you are best at. Find someone else to do the links that you are not good at as well as lower-value work.

3. Here is a simplified example of breaking down a business into the develop-make-tell-sell processes. Imagine an outfit that you bought for $100. In the develop stage, the company's in-house designer designed the clothes for $5. In the make stage, the company paid an outside factory to produce the clothes for $20.

4. In the tell stage, the company hired a marketing agency to create splashy ads for $20. In the sell stage, the company allowed retailers to make $50 to stock and sell the clothing. That all adds up to $95. If the product sells for $100, then the clothing company makes a $5 profit.

A. Break your business down into a value chain: develop, make, tell, and sell. Which step creates the most value? The least value? Can a particular process be outsourced? Don't worry if you don't know all the answers. The goal is to identify gaps by thinking through all your business steps.

B. Estimate the cost of each step, and compare that to how much you can actually sell the product or service. Profit = Sales price less Cost. In brief, you need to create value to sustain your dream—in this case, to keep producing and selling your product or service. Mapping out the value chain is a great way to identify gaps and to determine what needs to be done.

VALUE CHAIN

DEVELOP
What is idea?
Write product brief
Test with friends
Test with customers
Make prototype
Test with friends
Test with customers
Make final prototype
Outsource prototyping?

MAKE
Product:
Make inhouse or outsource?
Raw materials needed?
Facility and equipment?
Labor?
Packaging
Time to make product?
Guestimate costs

TELL
Who is customer?
How do they decide?
What is message?
How do I reach customer?
What marketing do you need?

SELL
What is sales process?
What are realistic measurements?
What sales force is needed?

 EXAMPLES

Alex made a living as a textile designer but wanted to be involved in what he considered to be his true love: running. He had been a competitive runner through college, but earning a living took him in different directions. He now designed fabrics for home furnishings using computer-aided design and digital printers. Alex saw the opportunity in running wear as he hated what the big companies offered. He liked the technical fabrics that have moisture-wicking properties and are soft to the touch. But all the clothes they sold were in black, red, neon yellow, and blue. He wanted to design retro-looking running clothes using a technical fabric so that consumers could get the best of both worlds.

Alex broke down the business into the four processes (create, make, sell, and tell). He could design the prints on his computer, and the digital printing could be done with the folks from his day job. He contacted a sports fabric company to check lead times and pricing.

Most importantly, Alex talked to his running buddy Jon, who worked as a senior manager at a large running retailer. Alex ran the numbers to see if he could make a small batch of technical running gear. His margins were lower than usual, but he would not have to do much inventory because the product could be made to order. Alex and Jon agreed to try the product in three stores to see if the product would sell. Maybe this could work.

Don wanted to do something more. He worked at an ad agency after working for a bicycling magazine. He had covered cyclocross racing, which is currently the fast growing segment in bicycling. He had a personality conflict with the magazine owner and left. But, he still loved cyclocross. He saw that other bicycling segments—road, triathlon, and mountain biking—had social networks, which made money by selling through online advertising.

Don broke down the business into create, make, tell, and sell. First, he asked a co-worker how much building a website would cost. He checked with freelance bicycling journalists to see if they were interested in writing articles at a friends-and-family rate. Don contacted regional cyclocross race organizers to gauge their support. Finally, he contacted his friends at the bicycle and accessories companies to check their rates for advertising on a cyclocross-dedicated website.

Don put together a budget and looked into his own finances. He thought he could start the business as a hobby, and then he and his girlfriend, a police officer, could live off her salary for a while. After mapping the whole chain, he thought it might be worth a shot to create a social network.

Margaret considered opening a high-end houseware store in her home town. She wanted to sell to affluent tourists. She mapped out the retail process. Margaret could use her previous vendors to get favorable terms to purchase products. She would cut a deal with her uncle who was in the process of closing a general store at a good location in town. She offered 30% of her business for two years of free rent and $60K in working capital. Margaret would find employees who were moms that found it hard to find jobs.

When she put a budget together, she realized that she would have to mark up products 2.2 to 2.5 times, or 60% gross profit margin, to make the economics work. She knew that those price points wouldn't work for locals but would work for the tourists. She also considered that the tourist season was only nine months long. After mapping out the business, she felt that it had a good chance of being profitable.

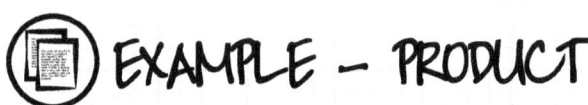 EXAMPLE – PRODUCT

PRODUCT EXAMPLE: ALEX'S RUNNING APPAREL

DEVELOP
Find technical fabric
Write product brief
Select prints
Show brief to friends and buyers
Make sample and swatches
Show sample to buyers
Get pricing
Make final samples

MAKE
Product:
Get fabric terms
Calculate equipment prices
Decide location
Who can make?
Get packaging
Time to make product?
Guestimate costs

TELL
Customer: Runners and store buyer
Research how they buy
Message: Retro rocks with techno
Website and sponsorship

SELL
Target other running stores
What are realistic measurements?
Independent vs inhouse sales force

EXAMPLE – SERVICE

SERVICE EXAMPLE: DON'S CYCLOCROSS WEBSITE

DEVELOP	MAKE
Test website with industry	Find freelance writers and cost
Find web developer	Get bike product release info
Develop website	Raw materials needed?
Website cost and lead time	How maintain website
Test with friends	Costs?

TELL	SELL
Develop customer profile	Define sales process
Decide message	Set customer list
Develop press kit	Decide on customer force
Develop contract	What are measurements?

FAQ

1. **What if I don't know all the steps?** Don't worry. This is the first step in trying to fill out what needs to be done. This tool is for discovery, not drawing conclusions. This process will go a long way to identify what is missing.

INSTRUCTIONS

Overview: Break your business down into simple parts.
1. Answer the questions in each area: Create, Make, Tell and Sell.

VALUE CHAIN	
DEVELOP	**MAKE**
What is idea?	Product:
Write product brief	Make inhouse or outsource?
Test with friends	Raw materials needed?
Test with customers	Facility and equipment?
Make prototype	Labor?
Test with friends	Packaging
Test with customers	Time to make product?
Make final prototype	Guestimate costs
Outsource prototyping?	
Fill in answers below.	
DEVELOP	**MAKE**
TELL	**SELL**
Who is customer?	What is sales process?
How do they decide?	What are realistic measurements?
What is message?	What sales force is needed?
How do I reach customer?	
What marketing do you need?	
Fill in answers below.	
TELL	**SELL**

THINK

Team Building

Identify your strengths and weaknesses and build a team to deal with them accordingly.

Watch Video
www.joestartup.com/module/think/teamwork

A. Team building is another area that is often neglected in a small business. Most likely, you can't be the best at everything. Do a reality check on what you are capable of doing, and build a team around that capability.

B. Teams build great businesses. To use a basketball analogy, it is nearly impossible for one player to play a point guard, center, and small forward. So, pay attention to your strengths and weaknesses and build a business team around them.

C. Find a partner who is really good in areas in which you are weak. A partner is great for sharing the overwhelming workload and experience. Besides a partner, you will also need to find role players to do lower-value work or other work in which you are inexperienced.

D. In the beginning, you may have to do most of the work, but you must ask for help from friends and family. Find help in the areas where you feel limited in terms of practical knowledge and inspiration. Ask these questions: Are you good with people? Do you work with numbers easily?

Do you like telling stories on paper or through pictures? Many small businesses get stuck between wanting to have more help to grow but lacking the money to hire help. Business owners hope to get things done by themselves. Using the value chain, you can better estimate where to invest in help in the form of outsourcing work or finding a capable employee to make a big difference.

Take small chances by testing out an employee for a fixed term. Carefully consider your strengths and weaknesses as well your business' value chain. Do something about it.

Here is an example: Elana is an outgoing individual with a million ideas. Her friend Ellie is also a people person and is imaginative. Peter, on the other hand, loves solving problems and prefers numbers to people. Elana knows she needs Peter and his skills for troubleshooting and for the financial aspect of the business. Elana will be good at conceptualizing and interacting with customers, while Peter will make sure that actual details get done.

Elana really likes Ellie's imagination but is worried that they may clash because of their personalities. She needs to think how to clearly define responsibilities and decision making if she works with Ellie.

Write out the strengths and weaknesses of your team. What skills are you missing? Do you need them full time or temporarily? Identify the gaps in your processes, and find people to help fill them.

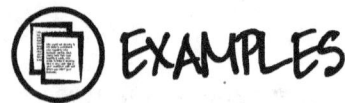 EXAMPLES

Brett loved bees but hated selling honey. The hive got bigger and bigger. There was so much that Brett could not give the honey away. Friends always suggested that he sell honey at the farmer's market or at the local tourist shops. Brett would have none of that. He was a bee person, not a people person. One day, his nephew Milo asked if they could start a business called Sippin' Bee Honey.

Brett knew that Milo had a silver tongue and charmed his way through life. Brett agreed to keep the bees, while Milo would hit the farmer's markets and local tourist shops and then build a simple website. Both brought different skills to the business.

Greg was just laid off from his position as an agricultural economist conducting research on wheat. Fewer research economist jobs were available as states were cutting their staff in the downturn. Greg knew everything there was to know about wheat markets. He didn't want to move because of family reasons.

In a chance meeting, Greg ran into Pete, a high school classmate, at a coffee shop. Pete had just moved back to his hometown after a successful career in big data stock trading. In his previous job, he developed computer programs that analyzed enormous amounts of data and made stock trades. While Greg and Pete were never close, both understood that each had different skills sets. They decided to develop a big data wheat trading program. If they had some success, they would ask Charlie, another classmate and stock broker, to help identify investors.

Courtney, a retired ballerina, and Sally were not friendly in high school. Years later, Courtney would often run into Sally who had children that were the same age as her own. They were opposites. Courtney was free-spirited and loved dancing, while Sally was good at math and was usually by the book. As adults, they got along as they shared mothering experiences.

On a warm summer day, Sally complained that there was no dance studio where her children could learn dancing. She suggested that Courtney start a dance studio. Courtney, however, knew many successful dancers who failed at dance studios. One of the reasons for the failure was the lack of understanding that dance was only one part of establishing and running a studio. So, Courtney said she would only be interested if Sally was a partner. Courtney knew that Sally had experience in administrative tasks but was tired of preparing tax returns for customers. They both agreed to talk about it at the next play date.

? FAQ

How do I find the right people?

The best way to start is by carefully determining and writing out your business needs. Then, ask friends and advisors for suggestions. Get more details later in the Right People module.

(i) INSTRUCTIONS

Overview: Identify your strengths and weaknesses, and build a team accordingly.

Answer the following questions in several paragraphs.

1. Write out the strengths and weaknesses of your team.

_____
_____
_____
_____
_____
_____
_____
_____

2. What skills are you missing?

_____
_____
_____
_____

3. Do you need them full time or on a temporary basis?

_____
_____
_____

THINK

Enterprise Haiku

Create a clear roadmap by making tradeoffs.

Watch Video
www.joestartup.com/module/think/enterprise-haiku

A. My friend Dave asked how to rise above the chaotic fog of running an under-resourced business. The first step is to distill the business essentials and build a specific plan around them.

B. The Haiku is the essential roadmap to what an enterprise needs to do. Don't worry if you don't know all the answers immediately.

Identify the gaps. Find answers from online research, friends, advisors, and potential users.

C. The Enterprise Haiku captures key trade-offs on one page. Revise this sheet as many times as needed after talking with as many advisors and potential users as possible. This document will be a great preparation to grow a business.

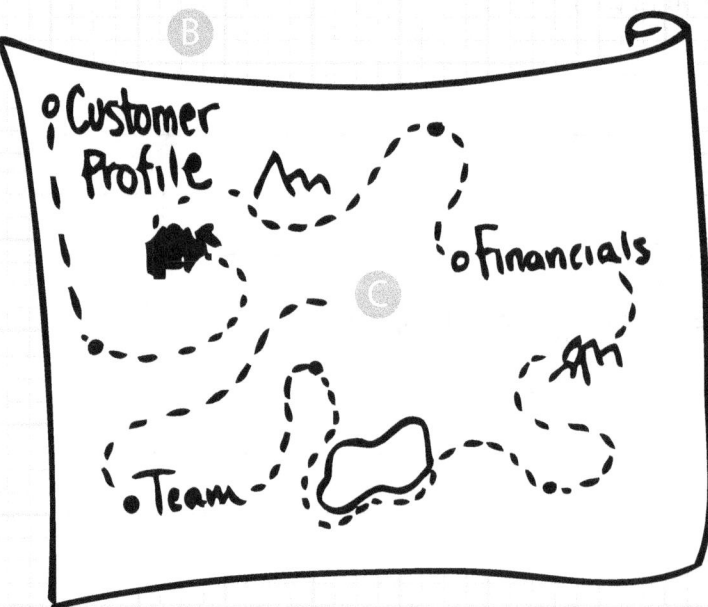

EXAMPLES - PRODUCT

PRODUCT HAIKU — *distill more to less...*

IDEA - A super fun board and card game where players race to build a house profitably

customer cheatsheet

	#1	#2
customer type	kids 9-18	parents of kids 9-18
greatest need	fun game	education & fun for family
most important benefits: #1		
#2		
#3		
where buy	website & Amazon	website & Amazon
competitors	None	None
ABD: price, product, cust serv	Best product, unique	Best product
avg yearly purchased units		10,000
avg price		25
avg annual purchase amt		25
# potential customer		10,000,000
potential market size		250,000,000

customer path / marketing materials

customer path	marketing materials	marketing materials
website	website	website
Amazon	social media	social media
independent toy stores		PR in parenting magazines

value chain

create	make	tell	sell
board/card design	outsource manufacturing	website	website
		parent/kid social media	Amazon
		homeschooling	

first customers
- Local kids
- Local boyscouts
- Local YMCA
- Local independent toy store
- Homeschool association

sales cycle
- Email/Adwords
- Website visit
- Website purchase/Amazon

key dates
- Complete design brief 2/1
- Prototype 3/1
- Finalize 5/1
- First product delivery 6/15
- Live website & Amazon 7/1

message
Crazy fun in learning how to build a home

open questions
1. How do I get the word out cost effectively?
2. How do I design the graphics & rules so it is crazy fun?
3. How do I sell through Amazon
4. How do I develop social media?
5. How do I manage outsourced manufacturing?

funding sources
1. Self funding
2. Friends & Family
3. Indiegogo

need most help
1. Design help
2. Game makers
3. Website design

breakeven analysis - monthly

# Units Sold	600
Avg. Sales Price	25
Total Sales (# Units X Price)	15,000
Create - Product Costs	4,000
Tell - Marketing Expenses	3,000
Run - People Expenses	7,000
Other Expenses	1,000
Total Costs	15,000
Cash Flow	0
Development expenses	10,000
Months-to-Breakeven	5
Cash needed until breakeven	20,000

SERVICE — EXAMPLES

SERVICE HAIKU

IDEA - A content rich marketplace for 3D printers where ebay meets consumer reports and Design

customer cheatsheet	#1	#2	first customers
customer type	Industrial designers & prototyping	Individual Maker Movement	Chicago Prototyping Inc.
greatest need	content rich, trusted marketplace	content rich, trusted marketplace	US Prototyping
most important benefits:_____ #1			APD Inc.
#2			
#3			
where buy	online	online	**sales cycle**
competitors	word of mouth	ebay	Conference word of mouth
ABD: price, product, cust serv	Best product: content rich	Best product: content rich	Online ads in targeted trade pubs
avg yearly purchased units	1	1	Website visit
avg price($K)	30,000	1,500	
avg annual purchase amt($K)	30,000	1,500	
# potential customer	4,000	50,000	**key dates**
potential market size	120,000,000	75,000,000	Design brief 3/1
customer path	**marketing materials**	**marketing materials**	Launch beta 9/1
online marketplace	email	Adword	Prototyping comp program 10/1
	Adword	Print advertising in Maker Mag	Leave current day job 12/31
	brochure		

value chain

create	make	tell	sell
design brief	develop website	email	direct calls on top
wireframes		adwords	100 prototyping companies
user group feedback		Indiegogo campaign	
		PR	
		brochure/print advertising	

message

Easy, one stop shopping of 3D printers

breakeven analysis - monthly

# Units Sold	17
Avg. Sales Price X 10%	2,100
Total Sales (# Units X Price)	35,700
Create - Product Costs	
Tell - Marketing Expenses	10,000
Run - People Expenses	20,000
Other Expenses	5,000
Total Costs	35,000
Cash Flow	700
Development expenses	65,000
Months-to-Breakeven	6
Cash needed until breakeven	85,000

open questions
1. Use existing marketplace software?
2. How to ensure financial security?
3. How develop vibrant community?
4. How do we develop broad prototyping company relationships?
2. How to ensure financial security?

funding sources
1, Self funding

2. Indiegogo
3

need most help
1. Proto shop relationships

2. Online community development
3. Marketplace software

(i) INSTRUCTIONS

Overview: The Enterprise Haiku is the roadmap of tradeoffs needed to create a sustainable business.
1. Fill in the template below. Don't worry if you don't know all the answers now. Make a best guess and revise later.

ENTERPRISE HAIKU

IDEA -

customer cheatsheet	#1	#2	first customers
customer type			
greatest need			
most important benefits: ___ #1			
#2			
#3			
where buy			sales cycle
competitors			
ABD: price, product, cust serv			
avg yearly purchased units			
avg price			
avg annual purchase amt			
# potential customer			key dates
potential market size			
customer path	marketing materials	marketing materials	

value chain

create	make	tell	sell

message		breakeven analysis - monthly	
		# Units Sold	
		Avg. Sales Price	
open questions		Total Sales (# Units X Price)	
1		Create - Product Costs	
2		Tell - Marketing Expenses	
3		Run - People Expenses	
4		Other Expenses	
5		Total Costs	
funding sources	**need most help**	Cash Flow (Sales less Costs)	
1	1	Development expenses	
2	2	Months-to-Breakeven	
3	3	Cash needed until breakeven	

THINK

Presentation
Create a tool to communicate effectively.

Watch Video
www.joestartup.com/module//think/presentation

A. My friend John asked me how to put together a presentation for potential advisors and partners and how to do a presentation for investors.

B. I explained that one well-done presentation that is updated regularly can serve many different audiences.

C. The key is to keep the presentation updated and add or subtract pages depending on the target audience.

EXAMPLE – PRODUCT

Ironhorse Granola
Strong-like-bull endurance recovery

Create - Product Summary

Ironhorse Granola is a succulent mixture of high quality carbohydrates, protein, antioxidants and natural anti inflamatory to facilitate short cycle recoveries

Athletes will improve fitness more quickly with enhanced recoveries aka "Strong like bull!" Oh yeah, it tastes awesome too.

Formulations done by nationally-ranked endurance athletes, D1 collegiate athletes & cyclocrossers who have many years experience in nutritional supplements, formulas and pharmaceuticals-Where science meets the road

Tell - Customer Experience

Customer: Endurance Athletes & wanna bes

Customer hears about product at events & word of mouth

Shorter, high quality recoveries is problem solved

Improved fitness and great taste are key benefits

Customers buy at events, website and eventually running/cycling stores

Tell - Opportunity

Cereal and snack bar market is $1.7 billion

Customer currently buying other granolas & bars

Competitors: Naked Bear, Kashi, Cascadian, local brands

Differentiators: Special recovery formulation, yummy & funny ads

Key message: Improve fitness through enhanced recovery formulation

Tell - Opportunity

Cereal and snack bar market is $1.7 billion

Customer currently buying other granolas & bars

Competitors: Naked Bear, Kashi, Cascadian, local brands

Differentiators: Special recovery formulation, yummy & funny ads

Key message: Improve fitness through enhanced recovery formulation

Run - Key Processes

Key processes: Development, Manufacturing, Marketing, Sales

Open questions:
1. Taste vs cost balance
2. Enough margin
3. Ability to scale

Next steps:
1. Develop first batch 1 December
2. Sampling Jan cx races

Run - Management Team

Dr. John Speed CEO & Chief Product Officer *serial entrepreneur, pharma maven, nat ranked triathlete, competitive sailor, cyclocrosser*

Bill Maker VP Sales & Marketing *nutritional supplements & formula developer, triathlete, soccer player & cyclocrosser*

Run - Financial Summary

Year 1 sales and profits are $50K and $8K

Company breaks even in 8 months

Total investment is $7K

Return to investor is 18%

The Ask

Sample batches with cost analysis to determine viability

THINK

 EXAMPLE – SERVICE

The BAD Group
Big Algorithm Data Developers

Create - Product Summary
Algorithms tailored for specific trading markets. BAD algorithms identify anomalies in different ways. Investment strategies are developed using these anomalies

Products
1. Proprietary trading
2. Service model to sell to hedge funds

BAD has developed custom algorithms balanced with human judgement to create human/machine model

Tell - Customer Experience
Customer: In house & hedge funds

BAD Group very selective about potential clients. Referrals will drive the business. Key account list of 50 is first target

The problem solved is creating a profitable trading strategy by identifying the signal in the noise

Key customer benefit: Client makes money using blending algorithm/human model

Key accounts calls to select clients

Tell - Opportunity
Market size is gigantic. First markets: Emerging markets

Key competitors: Hedge funds and big data traders

Differentiators: Algorithms & market savvy traders

Key message: Combining big data algorithms with human judgement takes full advantage of all info available

Sell - Distribution
Sell method(customer path): Inhouse sales force

Sales process:
1. Word of mouth referrals
2. Initial pitch
3. Validation data sets
4. Customized trading strategy
5. Contract signing

Key sales measurements: Signed Contracts/Pitches, Signed contracts/Validation presentations

Sales force type: High service key accounts

Run - Key Processes
Key processes: Relevant market validation, Algorithm Development, Trading, Sales & Customer Maintenance

Open questions:
1. Does algorithm create signal to facilitate profitable trading strategy given volatile marketing conditions

Next steps:
1. Complete v1 validation in select emerging markets
2. Determine which markets algorithm delivers best
3. Modify algorithm

Run - Management Team
Dr. Jim Start Big data/algorithm guru and econometrician

David Stock Equity research analyst, fund manager

Peter Sellers equity trader and sales manager

Run - Financial Summary
Company breaks even and supports 6 staff in 10 months

Total investment is $350K

Return to investor is 44%

The Ask
Identify traders to help determine anomalies and develop investment strategies

Raise $10 million fund among 15 investors by June

 FAQ

1. **What if I don't have the answers?** Don't worry; you will learn more as you progress through the Joe Startup plan. The presentation is the starting point and will evolve into a finished product.

2. **What if I prefer Prezi presentations?** We encourage you to build the presentation in Google, and copy over to Prezi (www.prezi.com) when you feel that the time is right.

 INSTRUCTIONS

Overview: Draw up a presentation to learn about business, and communicate with team members, potential advisors, and investors.

1. In the Google presentation, answer the questions on each slide. Feel free to add/delete.

2. The presentation is a process. You will probably not have all the answers on day 1. Update as you complete the Joe Startup Checkup.

3. Share with potential team members, advisors, and investors.

CREATE - PRODUCT SUMMARY

What is the product / service?
___
___

How it is developed and made?
___
___

TELL - CUSTOMER EXPERIENCE

Who is customer?
___
___

How customer finds out about product?
___
___

What problem solved?
___
___

Key customer benefit?
___
___

Key customer buys?
___
___

TELL - OPPORTUNITY
Market size: _____
_____

How is problem being solved today? _____
_____
_____

Key competitors: _____
_____
_____

Differentiators: _____
_____
_____

SELL - DISTRIBUTION
Customer path (channel) _____
_____

How is problem being solved today? _____
_____
_____

Sales process: _____
_____
_____

Key sales measurements: _____
_____
_____

Sales force type: _____
_____
_____

RUN - KEY PROCESSES
Key processes: (Development, Manufacturing, Marketing, Sales)
_____
_____
_____

How is problem being solved today?
_____
_____
_____

RUN - FINANCIAL SUMMARY
Year 1 sales and profits are _____ and _____
_____
_____

Company breaks even in __ months
_____
_____
_____

Total investment is $ _____
_____
_____
_____

Return to investor is __ %
_____
_____
_____

THE ASK
What help are you looking for? (advice, money)
_____
_____

CREATE

Creative Mindset

A creative mindset requires structure and exercises.

Watch Video
www.joestartup.com/module//dream/creative-mindset

Most small business owners need to be creative in order to develop new products/services. Owners also need to cultivate such divergent thinking to identify novel solutions to their current problems.

A. My friend Randee says that she is not creative. I disagree. When she was 9 years old, I imagine that I would see someone incredibly curious, creative, and hungry to learn. Somehow, our education system dims those qualities.

B. In my mind, everyone has a creative talent. It just needs to be rediscovered. It is like a muscle that has not been used. It needs to be nurtured and strengthened by using it every day.

D. Even improvisational comedy follows rules to facilitate the creation of funny scenes. In short, we need a framework and the right mindset to produce creative outcomes. A few exercises will help.

C. We often hear how athletes are "in the zone" where everything just flows naturally. For artists and writers, it seems ideas present themselves almost as gifts, that is, with little effort. The reality is that getting "in the zone" usually happens when there is a mindset, a structure, and lots of practice.

CREATE

A. Imagine that you are a spy and that you have to memorize all the details of a room. What is the paint's color? What is the trim like? Where is the light coming from? In this exercise, focus on the present moment.

B. Every day, look for inspiration. An interesting artwork or design can help you understand what is out there and help you define what you want. Cool products and businesses on Indiegogo or Kickstarter can inspire you. Record interesting and creative ideas in a journal to use as a source of inspiration.

C. Don't pressure yourself to come up with the one great idea. Most successful ideas are mash-ups of previous ideas. Pablo Picasso said "good artists copy, great artists steal." The iPhone is literally a mash-up of a phone, a music player, and computer apps.

D. eBay is an auction (a several-hundred-year-old idea) applied online. In fact, many great concepts are ideas from one field applied to another. So, remix ideas from one part of life and apply them to another.

E. Doing these exercises regularly will help you get in the creative zone. Many ideas will present themselves to you. Be willing to entertain a number of bad ideas to come up with a few good ideas. Put yourself out there believing that the process will ultimately yield good results.

CREATE

1. Make a "what makes me frustrated" list. Think about badly solved or unsolved problems at home, work, or elsewhere. What solutions—products or services—could you offer to deal with these problems?

2. For example, city dwellers desperately wanted to use cars for errands or short trips. The solution provided was short-term rental cars parked in convenient city locations. List other people's frustrations.

3. Set aside creative time every day. It could be as little as 15 minutes to several hours. Review your inspiration journal.

The first time will seem hard, but like working a muscle, creativity will come easier if you are consistent. Creativity requires consistency and structure for great ideas to appear.

4. When the day is busy, stop and count 10 breaths. This pause will help you concentrate on the moment.

5. Keep a hobby that makes the mind wander — a type of activity that allows the brain to process life's details. Ideally, observe your thoughts without forming attachments or feelings. Try an exercise or a hobby that allows or encourages you to focus on the present moment and nothing else.

 EXAMPLES

Abe, a controller at a tech company, wondered if things could be different at work. He and his wife, a graphic artist at a product prototyping company, spent a lot of time with designers. Abe was convinced that he was not very creative; he preferred the comfort of numbers and rigid processes.

Late one evening at a dinner party, his wife's boss, a well-known design guru, shared a secret: Creativity is a mindset. He explained that Abe has a domain—or specific—knowledge about certain subjects. Abe should use this expert knowledge to look for unsolved needs and solve them in new ways, perhaps from another perspective. His wife's boss suggested that he keep a notebook of unsolved needs and inspirations. Enthused, Abe let his mind wander during his daily runs.

Benny, a general contractor, wanted to do something different. The last few years had been tough. He spent more time with his kids while his wife worked as a nurse. With the economic slowdown, he had more time to think about things. He started mountain bike riding again to get healthy. On the trail, he met folks with completely different backgrounds—accountants, gaming consultants, and teachers. He often came up with ideas but forgot them until he started writing notes in his contractor notebooks.

Benny kept finding himself coming back to one thing: that he enjoyed playing board games or cards with his kids. One day while playing Monopoly, he thought, "why not create a game where kids are racing to build a house?" Benny wondered if he could create a game that is fun and teaches kids how to build houses.

Eli, a plumber, needed a change. Since 2009, business had fallen off dramatically. The business had changed, and there were lots of plumbers in the resort town in which he lived. Most of his friends shrugged when he asked for advice.

One day, he rode his Harley-Davidson to a motorcycle rally. That day, strangers were kind, and he picked up tidbits on motorcycles and life. On the long ride home, he remembered the advice about keeping your eyes open for badly solved problems and keeping notes. He heard a lot of complaints that day, but none clicked. Eli committed to the idea of spending at least 30 minutes a day looking for something new.

 **FAQ**

1. **What if I am not really creative?** Creativity is a mindset and a process. It is true that some people are more predisposed to creative endeavours. However, even the most creative people have a process so they get work done on their uninspired days. It takes practice, like everything else.

2. **Where do I find sources of inspiration?** Depends on what you want your enterprise to do. Besides the really practical Indiegogo and Kickstarter for products and services, it could be medical journals or trade publications. It could be more general inspiration like Pinterest or Etsy or Instagram. Follow your passion on the web, and in journals and magazines. Inspiration can come from anywhere.

 **INSTRUCTIONS**

Overview: A creative mindset requires structure and exercises

Be in the present moment and open to opportunities. Do the exercises regularly.

1. Keep a journal of inspirational products and services.

2. Create a "what makes me frustrated" list of unmet needs.

INSPIRATIONAL PRODUCTS & SERVICES

_____
_____
_____
_____
_____
_____
_____
_____
_____
_____

WHAT MAKES ME FRUSTRATED LIST

NOTES

CREATE

Innovation Process
The acronym PRICE, Problem Research, Ideation, Curating, and Editing.

Watch Video
www.joestartup.com/module//think/presentation#

A. Small business owners often tell me that they are not creative enough to come up with many cool ideas. But what does it really mean to be creative? Creativity is the ability to see and convey ideas or emotions in new ways. Innovation is applied creativity, or the process of focusing creativity to produce a solution where the author or others see value. A solution may come in the form of a product or a service.

B. Innovation is a process of channeling creativity into finding and creating solutions. It can be done individually or through group effort. Let us take a look at the five steps (PRICE) in the innovation process.

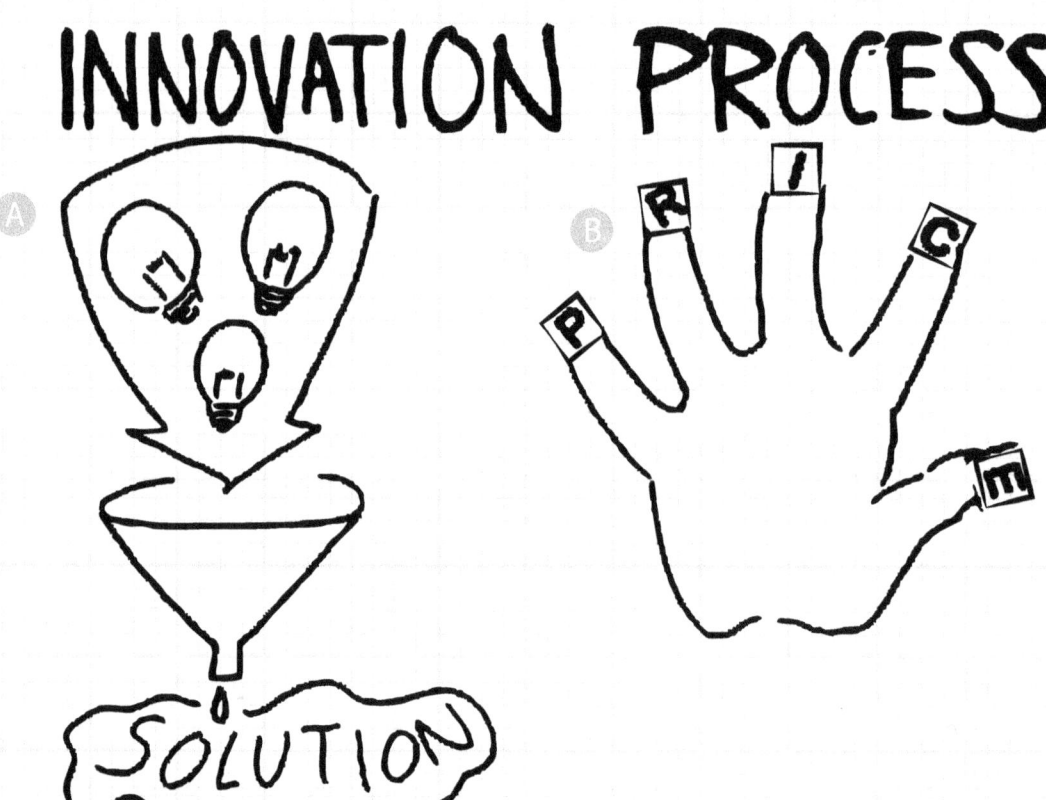

1. Problem identification: Clearly lay out the problem and the key frustrations related to it. Finish the phrase "I don't like that..." Get as much feedback as you can from potential users. Learn more about their environment and perceptions to help you understand the problem and therefore be able to formulate an appropriate solution. In the end, it's all about the users and how your solution addresses their concerns.

2. Research: Conduct research on the problem, the available solutions, and the solution providers. Understand the landscape clearly. Google solution providers and talk to customers. Pretend that you are a detective looking for all possible options. Skipping this process may lead to a duplication of a concept, a product, or a service that already exists. With proper research, on the other hand, you can avoid wasting time and effort. With enough accurate information, you can focus on finding gaps and understanding current inadequacies in current solutions, if there are any, and then start developing a better solution.

3. Ideation: Think of as many potential solutions as you can. Be messy. Overshoot on the ideas. Write them down no matter how crazy they may seem. Don't be critical in this stage; just come up with a ton of ideas. When you get stuck, ask "What if?" to keep going.

4. Curating: Study the potential solutions side by side, and consider ways to combine them. Leave all options on the table, and remix the ideas. Then, start classifying and identifying the best concepts.

5. Editing: Eliminate ideas based on benefits, costs, and feasibility. Distill your options down to the most realistic solution with the highest value.

6. The PRICE process can be cumbersome and awkward. You might be tempted to edit before you are done with the ideation and curating steps. Keep in my mind, though, that innovation takes time. It does not follow a straight line; it zigs and zags. Be patient and keep practicing. Often, the process involves building layers on top of each other.

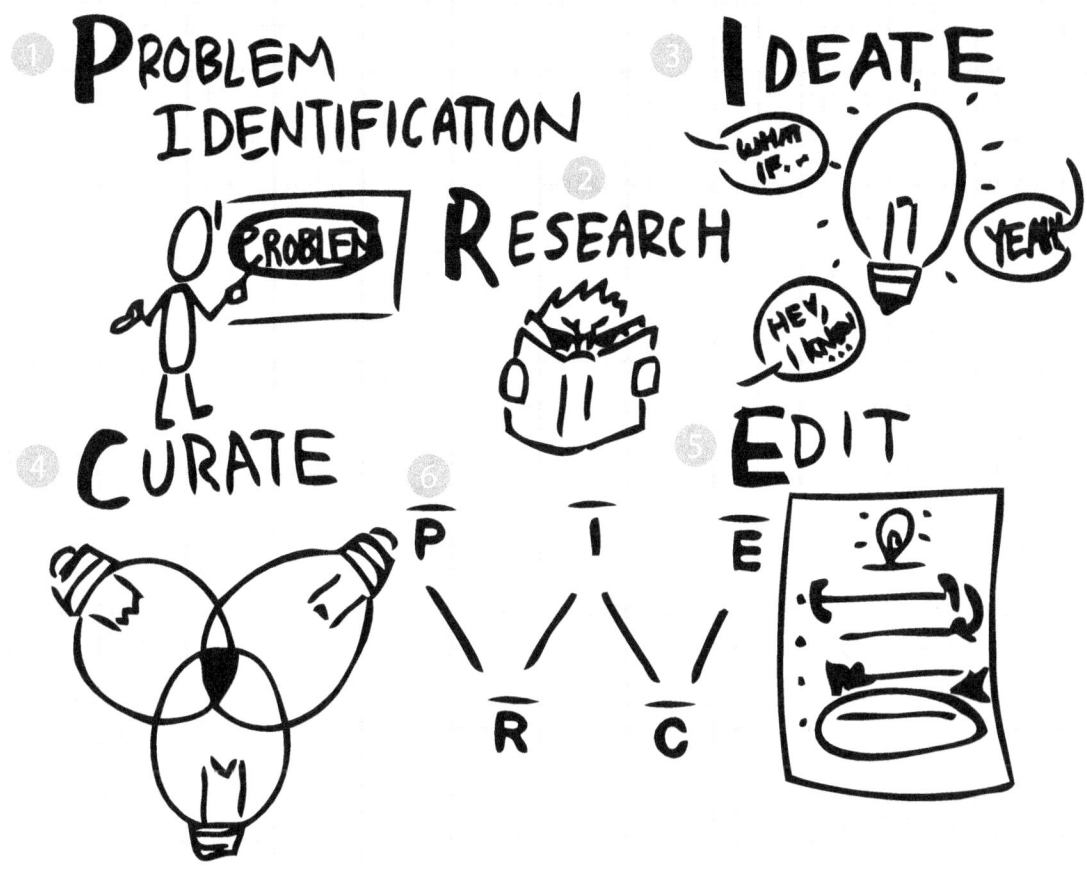

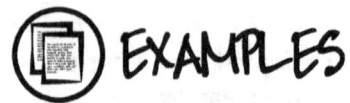 **EXAMPLES**

Abe, a financial controller, had kept a notebook on unmet needs. He and his wife hung out with designers and product development people. In addition, Abe was a do-it-yourself (DIY) guy and enjoyed the Maker Movement. In both areas, 3D printing was really hot. The market was changing quickly with all the new introductions, both in personal and industrial printing. In short, there were people who wanted to start 3D printing without spending a fortune. There were people who wanted to sell their old printers so they could get new ones. The unmet need is in matching buyers and sellers.

Abe invited designers, prototyping people, and Maker Movement folks to a brunch meeting. He wanted to talk about the idea of a 3D-printer marketplace, an eBay for 3D printers that was heavy on content on all different choices. Abe had a list of questions, but he spent most of the time listening to what the potential users wanted. During the next two to three months, he met with as many potential users as he could.

Abe also researched how others were trying to develop a 3D-printer marketplace, paying attention to their strengths and shortcomings. He organized an ideation session with users, web development experts, and social network gurus. After the session, there were so many ideas. Next, he would have to classify and edit them to get a clear product definition.

Benny, a general contractor, had this fuzzy idea of a board game where kids could have fun by racing to build a house. He really wasn't sure what to do next. Benny watched his kids and friends play games and asked what they liked. He researched the games out there and purchased the ones that intrigued him. Benny wrote a ton of ideas in his notebook. After mashing up the best ideas, he asked his kids and their friends about the concept. He made changes. Benny then met with his friends—parents, teachers, and a video game designer. Benny made more changes. Finally, he got a friend to run a session with kids that he taught. Benny was ready to crystallize his idea into a product definition.

Eli, a plumber, had an idea, but it was murky. Todd, one of his better-off motorcycle buddies, complained about flooding damage to his house. As a favor, Eli took a look at the damage and the repair estimates. Todd complained that he paid a fortune and had to manage the plumber, electrician, and special cleaning crews. Todd explained that his neighborhood was in a floodplain, so there was often water damage. Eli asked if Todd could introduce him to neighbors with the similar concerns.

After reviewing their damages and estimates, Eli called the cleaning companies and found their service poor. He invited friends over to barbecue for a brainstorming session. Afterward, he sat with Bob, and they whittled the idea to a one-stop flood remediation service that offered plumbing, carpet cleaning, and electrical management. High-quality service at premium pricing is the service definition they worked toward. Eli thought he may be on to something.

 **FAQ**

1. **How do I identify the problem and user?** First, spend lots of time with the users of a product/service. Understand what they want and what motivates them. Empathize with them. How do they use the product/service? What are their likes and dislikes in relation to the product/service? Determine what they say their needs are versus what their actual needs are. Once needs are understood, then problems can be clearly identified.

2. **How do I do research?** The web is the best place to start. Do a product/service search. Look at competitor websites. Talk to current users, and ask their opinions on what they currently use. Search trade publications.

3. **How do I ideate?** Generating new ideas is much easier after understanding the problem and knowing what others have done to address the problem. Finish the statement "I can fix this better by..." Mull over the options. Step away from these ideas, and do something unrelated, like exercise, to give the mind time to process all the information. In addition, find out if other industries have solved similar problems and how. Group innovation sessions, which include people from different backgrounds, can be particularly helpful.

4. **How do I curate?** Go through all the ideas you have generated and present their advantages and disadvantages side by side. This could be on a pad of paper, a whiteboard, or Post-it notes. Pick the best options. Are there ways to combine some ideas to deliver a better solution?

5. **How do I edit?** Now is the time to eliminate options and to one. Use the Product Haiku to make needed tradeoffs and to distill your data into a concise product/service definition.

_____
_____
_____
_____
_____
_____
_____
_____
_____
_____
_____
_____
_____
_____

ⓘ INSTRUCTIONS

Overview: Use the acronym PRICE to develop the innovation process: Problem and user identification, Research, Ideate, Curate, Edit

Write out how you plan to develop your idea using PRICE. Include a list of open questions that need to be answered.

Product Haiku

Develop a clear product/service definition by making specific tradeoffs.

Watch Video
www.joestartup.com/module//dream/product-haiku

A. My friend Jim asked me how to turn a fuzzy idea into a new product or service. Ideas are like nuggets that have to be hammered, treated, and shaped to become a product. Ideas are often fuzzy and huge, while a successful product/service is defined clearly by making tradeoffs.

B. A clear product definition includes the problem you are trying to solve, who the user is, what the solution is, and its key features and benefits.

C. Once you have an idea, get the opinion of as many potential users as possible. The most common, and often disastrous, mistake is that entrepreneurs create products, services, and enterprises without getting input from the target users.

D. You should not assume that you know what the users want without actually checking with them first. Walk in their shoes. Understand their environment and what is important to them. Before finalizing a product or service definition, get the opinion of as many users as possible.

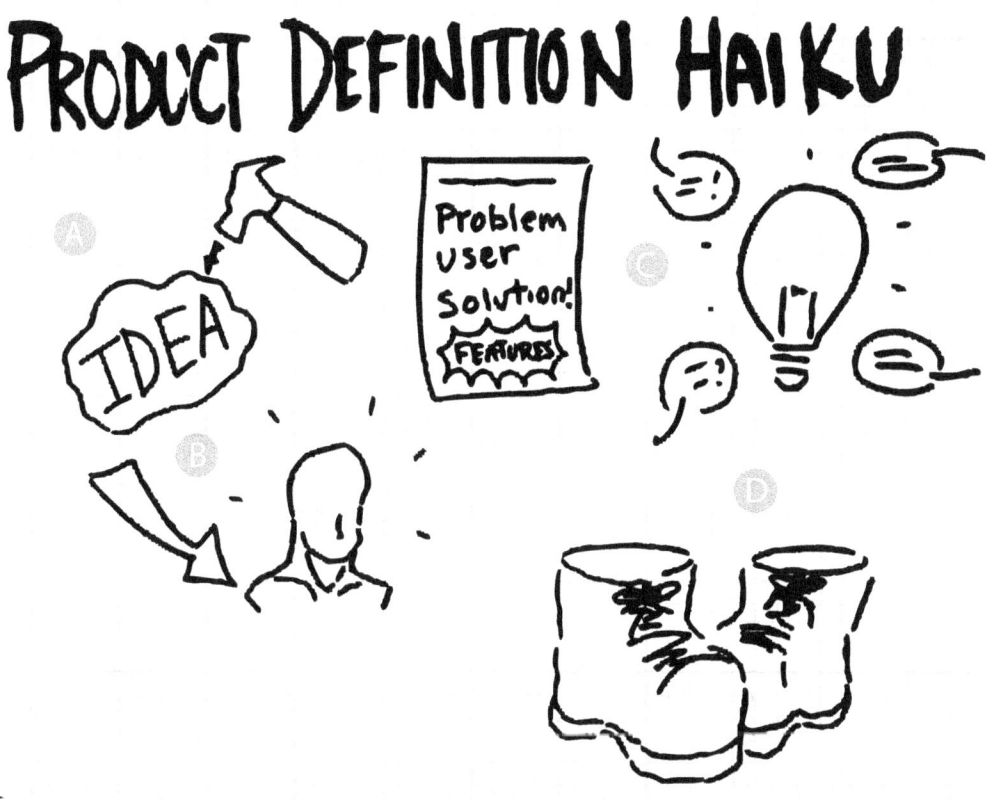

CREATE

1. A product definition involves a set of tradeoffs made so that you have a clear idea of what your product is and is not. With this clear definition, you can test the concept with as many users and advisors as possible.

2. Understand the user universe as much as you can. Creating new products and services requires a great deal of study, revision, and refinement well before you actually start making or selling.

PRODUCT HAIKU
distill more to less...

Problem		
User		
Solution		
Features	1	
	2	
	3	
	4	
	5	
Key benefits	1	
	2	
	3	
	4	
	5	
How different?		
Price		
How to develop & Where made?		
Next steps	1	
	2	
	3	
	4	
	5	

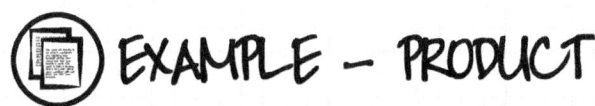 EXAMPLE – PRODUCT

PRODUCT HAIKU	PRODUCT	SERVICE
Problem	Develop games which are practical, educational and lots of fun	No marketplace for used 3D printers for industrial and personal users. Need a content given the diverse products and needs.
User	Kids 8-16	Two users: industrial users who are designers, prototyping shops and product development. In addition, personal users who are likely DIY and Maker Movement types.
Solution	A super fun board and card game where players race to build a house profitably	A content rich marketplace for 3D printers where ebay meets consumer reports and Design Magazine.
Features	1. Colorful board and cards	1. Easy-to-use marketplace software
	2. Education in bite sizes	2. Content of 3D printer basics
	3. Dice create chances and potential setbacks	3. Latest news feed
	4. Opportunities to collaborate with other players to create win-win situations	4. Library of downloadable object files
Key benefits	1. Teach kids the basics of general contracting in a fun, competitive way	1. Easy, one stop shopping for 3D printer
	2. Teach financial management skills	2. Well-curated content so users can make great buy/sell decisions
	3. Learn to deal with inevitable setbacks of bulding house	3. Sharing community to get answers to questions
How different?	No other similar games. There are real estate board games and financial management games but no edutainment games on building houses.	There are "dumb" non-specific marketplaces and incomplete content providers. No content rich marketplaces with community.
Price	$20 for card game, $35 for board game	10% on each transaction
How to develop & cost?	Hire graphic designer to develop print ready cards & board. Find manufacturer. Designer ($5K) Pilot cards ($1K) Pilot Board Game($3K)	Bring in inhouse web developer, develop base content from journalists. Cut $140K initial development budget to $25K by giving up equity. Commit $40K to marketing budget.
Where made?	Pilot order in US, Production order in Asia	Done by local web developer
Next steps	1. Hire graphic designer after developing design brief	1. Develop design brief
	2. Select card & board game manuacturer	2. Start developing content
	3. Decide distribution strategy	3. Develop marketing collateral to attract buyers/sellers
	4. Develop marketing plan	4. Develop site

 FAQ

What is the purpose of Haiku? Haiku will help you transform a fuzzy idea into a specific definition. This process will require making hard decisions. Keep in mind that you can change them later, but you will always have a clear definition.

What if I don't know the answers? In the beginning, you will not likely know all the answers. Research, think, and decide.

What do I do with Haiku? This is the critical first step to develop a product or service. Test this product/service definition with your potential users. After several refinements, you will be ready for prototyping.

CREATE

 **INSTRUCTIONS**

Develop a clear product/service definition by making specific tradeoffs.

Use the Product Haiku. Its structure will enable you to make the appropriate tradeoffs.

You will not likely know all the answers immediately. Research, think, and make decisions.

Complete the Haiku, keeping in mind that you can update it later with new information.

PRODUCT HAIKU	distill more to less…
Problem	
User	
Solution	
Features	1
	2
	3
	4
Key benefits	1
	2
	3
How different?	
Price	
How to develop & cost? Where made?	
Next steps	1
	2
	3
	4

Develop

Understand the development process.

Watch Video
www.joestartup.com/module//create/develop

A. My friend Brett asked me how to convert an idea into a real product or service. My answer is "TALK." Get user feedback. In the first stage, sketch out the idea, either through a drawing or a product description. What are the key features? What are the key benefits?

B. In the second stage, show a draft to friends, and ask for their opinions. What is the most important feature? What is the key benefit? What is lacking? Make necessary changes.

C. In the third stage, show a draft to target customers. Complete the customer profile module so that you can clearly define your target customer. Ask for their honest opinions. Rosy compliments will not help. Consider all suggestions, but only use those you feel are right.

D. In the fourth stage, make a prototype. Talk to the target customers. Read the reactions on their faces, and take note of what they say. Ask if they have other potential customers to introduce. Filter the comments and make more changes.

E. In the fifth stage, think how the suggested changes will affect the creation of the product or the service. Find a balance between what the target customers want, how easy it is to make, and how much it costs. Revise the prototype.

F. In the sixth stage, show prototypes to target customers you don't know. Ideally, you are selling the products even before they are made. Get these customers' honest opinions, and then revise the prototype. Now, you are ready to launch your product or service. Depending on the product or service, some steps in the development stage can be cut.

 EXAMPLES

Kit loved honey, especially that from the farmers market. But his love of honey would get him in trouble. When Kit ate honey, there was always a mess as the honey ran down the jar. His mother threatened to stop buying honey. When Kit complained, his father said he should do something about it. His father was an auto mechanic, so Kit was working on cars and welding in the shop even before he was a teenager. His mother, on the other hand, sold vegetables at the farmers market.

Kit went to the shop to create a no-mess cap. Several days later, Kit showed his parents a prototype. It didn't quite work, so Kit headed back to the shop. A week later, Kit went to the farmers market and talked to beekeepers. After asking several questions, he learned that he needed to make the product look better and to lower the price. The following week, Kit asked his father to take him to another farmers market to interview the honey sellers there. After tweaking the product for six weeks, he was able to develop a honey spout that honey sellers could buy for $2 and sell for $5. Having developed a new product, Kit was on his way to creating a business.

Don decided to start a cyclocross social network, but he had no idea how to design the website. He saw that the demand was there, but there were no websites. Don looked at the other social networks of triathlon, road riding, and mountain biking. His internet buddies stressed the importance of visual media, namely, being able to share lots of pictures. He put together a demo site with forums, blogs, and Facebook-like posts.

Don showed his cycling buddies and got their opinions—some useful, some useless. After making changes, he asked his friends to look at version 2. There were some ideas he could not afford, but he added a Pinterest and a Show-my-ride section to make the site more visual.

Don showed the website to some cyclocrossers whom he didn't know well, and he asked for their feedback. Finally, he showed it to potential advertisers to involve them in the design process. With all the feedback, he launched version 5 on the web. Don knew that there would be additional changes, but the customer-driven development process was the shortest and most cost-effective way to start.

After being in the jewelry business for 25 years, Roy finally came up with a blockbuster idea. He just wasn't exactly sure what the product and process would be. Roy knew that Facebook moms were his target, though, so he sent the product to a few friends. They gave lots of feedback, some of which he incorporated in his revision of the product. He asked those friends to make introductions to moms whom he did not know. Roy gave them a product in exchange for them filling out an online survey. More suggestions came through surveys. He tinkered with the product and process.

Roy offered free products to moms using a Facebook ad for three days, with the condition that they complete the online survey and speak with him by phone. When Roy looked at the online survey results, most suggestions were ones he had already considered. However, there were one or two new ideas that he liked and used. Roy felt ready to launch the new business after the development process.

 **FAQ**

1. How do I write a product summary? The easiest way to start a product summary is to explain what the product/service is to several friends. In the beginning, the description may seem clunky. After several explanations, write down the product summary to crystallize it. Then, show the written description to other friends and potential customers for more feedback.

2. What is a key benefit? A key benefit is the most-valued solution for the customer. For example, while an iPad has many features, many customers believe that the key benefit is that they can surf the web conveniently on the portable device. Or, for example, in a tree-cutting service, most customers see the key benefit as the tree cutter being dependable.

3. What is the difference between a feature and a benefit? A feature is a characteristic of a product, such as a TV having a 50-inch screen. A benefit is a solution that the product provides to the customer. For example, the 50-inch TV provides life-size viewing of sports.

4. What is a prototype? A prototype is a product sample before it goes into mass scale production.

5. What is a customer profile? A customer profile is a description of the essential characteristics of the customer. See more details in the Customer Profile module.

 **INSTRUCTIONS**

Overview: Understand the development process.

1. Describe the product and its key features in one to two paragraphs.

_____
_____
_____
_____

2. Include the key benefit, namely, the most valuable solution for the customer.

_____
_____

3. Ask friends and potential customers the following questions:
    a. What do they think of the product?
    b. What are the most important features of the product?
    c. What is the key benefit they see? What is lacking?
    d. How much would they pay for it?

4. Make reasonable product revisions.
5. Sketch or design a prototype.
6. Ask friends and potential customers the above questions on a sketch or prototype.
7. Presell the product if you can.

CREATE

Make

Learn about the overall making process for products and services.

Watch Video
www.joestartup.com/module//create/Make

A. My friend Milo, a chef, asked me how to move from product prototyping to manufacturing. It can seem so overwhelming. The change comes down to balancing control, complexity, and cost. Let's break down the production process into manageable stages.

B. First, determine the raw materials needed, where to get them lead times, costs, and minimum order quantities. Milo needs to check with a food distributor for these details. Second, determine the needed equipment and the facility. Where and how long does it take to get the equipment and complete renovations? How much does it cost? Milo must decide whether to upgrade his equipment or rent a commercial kitchen.

C. Third, identify who is going to make and package the product. How much training time is needed? How much time is needed for manufacturing? Milo needs to make a decision on whether to hire bakers or to train people.

D. Fourth, determine the time needed from receiving raw materials to finishing packaged goods. Calculate the material, labor, and facilities cost for one batch. Divide the total cost by the number of units to get an average product cost. So, if it costs Milo $100 to make 10 cakes, then the average cost is $10. He sets a sales price of $20.

E. Fifth, decide if the production process can be outsourced. Is it cheaper and faster than if you made the product? Outsourcing manufacturing can be easier, but you lose some control when you don't make the product. Who else could make the product? What is the cost, production time, and minimum order quantity?

F. After calculating the costs, Milo plans to talk to a nearby commercial bakery. He can make a final decision once he gets samples and costs. It may make sense to start manufacturing in-house and then outsource when you get bigger. Now you can understand the whole process.

G. Breaking down the production of a service is not much different from breaking down the manufacturing of a product. In addition to baking cakes, Milo arranges corporate events. First, there are typically no raw materials in services. Second, Milo needs to find vendors who rent tables, chairs, and tents as well as providers of food, beverages, and flowers. Also, he needs to know what venues to rent. Pricing and timing are important.

H. Third, identify who is going to perform the service. Milo needs to find waiters and how much they cost. Fourth, determine the expected time and cost needed from starting the project to service completion. Milo needs to make sure the numbers work for him and his customer.

I. Fifth, should the service be outsourced? Who else could provide the service? How much does it cost, what is the service time, and are there minimum commitments? Milo may outsource the food and beverage, except cakes, to a restaurant, which will make the project easier for him, although he will likely have to share the profit. To summarize, break down the work into manageable blocks. This process will help you make the tradeoffs between control, complexity, and cost.

Your new product/service introduction may not require all the steps of a full product introduction. Review the process and glean the needed steps.

? FAQ

1. **What is lead time?** This is the amount of time it takes to obtain raw materials or products once they have been ordered from the vendor.

1. **What are finished packaged goods?** These are final products that are packaged and ready to sell.

2. **What is average product cost?** It is calculated by dividing the total cost of materials, labor, equipment, and facilities by the number of products produced.

3. **What is labor?** Labor refers to the people needed to make the product.

4. **What is a vendor?** A vendor is a supplier or re-seller.

5. **What is control versus complexity?** This tradeoff relates to whether a business should outsource. Assuming that costs are equal, is the business willing to give up the control of production on premises versus eliminating the complexity of production on premises?

6. **What are minimum order quantities (MOQ)?** This is the minimum amount of ingredients that a vendor is willing to sell at a time.

7. **What are renovations?** Renovations are the changes that are needed in a facility to manufacture products.

8. **What is a batch?** A batch is the required amount to economically produce an item.

9. **What is a commercial kitchen and food distributor?** A commercial kitchen is a kitchen that people can rent out to make food to resell, while a food distributor is a reseller of food ingredients.

 EXAMPLES

Alex had much work to do. He received good news that a large running retailer wanted to test-market his apparel. Alex knew that his order quantities were too small to produce in China. His first calls were to U.S. sports textile companies to get terms, including pricing, minimum order quantities, and lead times on fabric.

Alex identified several U.S. cut-and-sew facilities. He knew the terms on digital printing. Alex put together a detailed budget and project plan. He would lose money on the first order but could make money on larger orders going forward. Alex decided to go ahead.

Rob was excited to create a new iPad app that was like a pinup poster for designers. Now, he had to turn it into reality. In the Create process, he showed his designer friends demo shots of the app and explained its functionality. Rob developed a design brief that defined the functional requirements and the look and feel of the app.

While listing the details was tedious, Rob found several things he missed. Rob also searched the web for app developers. He knew how to code, but some of the requirements were beyond his knowledge base. Rob sent out the design brief to three companies for bids. In the end, he did not go with the cheapest bid, but with one where he trusted the developers to get the job done right.

Steve wanted to create a commercial granola business that would be called Ironhorse Granola, but he didn't know how to make it in large quantities. Fortunately, one of his cycling buddies knew a baker who was willing to talk to him. The baker loved the idea and told him a list of what needed to be done.

Steve obtained the commercial kitchen rental rates and looked into the permits. He also got quotes—including price, minimum order quantity, and lead time—on cereal and from nut producers and packaging companies. Finally, he needed help, so he priced out the cost of getting baking assistants.

When he put all the numbers together, he realized that the business could have more money coming in than going out. The permits would take time, but he needed time to test larger-size batches. Ironhorse Granola might just work.

EXAMPLE - PRODUCT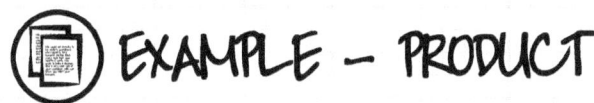

MILO'S CAKE BUSINESS

RAW MATERIALS & PACKAGING

Name	Cost	MOQ	Lead Time	Vendor
Bleached Flour	$45/50 pd bag	50 pd bag	1 week	Southern Baking
Wholewheat Flour	$49/50 pd bag	50 pd bag	1 week	Southern Baking
Eggs	$36/10 dozen	10 dozen	5 days	Bert's Eggs
Sugar	$72/50pd bag	50 pd bag	1 week	Southern Baking
Salt	$40/50 pd bag	50 pd bag	1 week	Southern Baking
Yeast	$25/5 pd	5 pd	10 days	Baker Specialty
Spices	$60/10pd	10 pd	20 days	Baker Spices
Cake plates	$100/unit	1000/unit	1 week	Baker Packaging
Cake boxes	$400/unit	1000/unit	1 week	Baker Packaging
Bows	$150/unit	1000/unit	1 week	Baker Packaging

EQUIPMENT LIST

Name	Cost		Lead Time	Vendor
Blender	$3,500		3 weeks	Titan Baking
Oven	$12,000		8 weeks	Hott Ovens
Cooling Racks	$2,200		2 weeks	Kol Racking
Pans	$2,800		1 week	Light Metalwerks
Shelving	$1,700		2 weeks	Light Metalwerks
Packaging Equipment	$1,200		4 weeks	Baker Packaging

FACILITIES COST

Name	Cost		Lead Time	Contractor
Oven bays			16	Titan Baking
Natural gas upfit			8	PNG
Clean floor			3	South Flooring
Sink Installation			4	Rush Plumbing
Lighting			3	Sky Lighting
Electrical upfit			2	Wolper Electrical

LABOR COST

Name	Cost			
Baker assistants	$18/hr inc SS			

EXAMPLE – SERVICE

MILO'S CATERING

LABOR COST

Name	Cost			
Waiters	$18/hr			
Bartenders	$25/hr			
DJ	$50/hr			

EQUIPMENT COST

Name	Cost		Lead Time	Contractor
Tables	$80/unit	10/unit	3 days	Party Specialty
Chairs	$60/unit	10/unit	3 days	Party Specialty
Dance Floor	$400/floor	1/unit	14 days	Party Specialty
Tents	$200/unit	1/unit	7 days	Smith Tents
Buffet Equipment	$110/unit	1/unit	5 days	Party Specialty
Dishes & Silverware	$40/unit	12 setting/unit	5 days	Party Specialty

INSTRUCTIONS

Overview: Learn the overall production process for products and services.

1. In the chart, list the raw materials (if needed), equipment, facility and labor.

2. Determine the product lead time from receiving raw materials to finishing packaged goods.

5. Calculate the average product cost.

6. Does it make sense to outsource production to someone else? If so, when?

PRODUCT COMPANY INPUT

RAW MATERIALS & PACKAGING LIST

Name	Cost	MOQ	Lead Time	Vendor

EQUIPMENT LIST

Name	Cost	Lead Time	Vendor

FACILITIES COST

Name	Cost	Lead Time	Contractor

LABOR COST

Name	Cost			

SERVICE COMPANY INPUT

LABOR COST

Name	Cost			

EQUIPMENT COST

Name	Cost	Lead Time	Contractor

CREATE

Process Map

Map out the processes and steps.

Watch Video
www.joestartup.com/module//create/process-map

My friend Alex, a running apparel designer, asked how he could possibly get everything done in his small business. He complained that there was too much to do in too little time. A process map will help you develop a step-by-step guide for managing the business. You will see the big picture, determine how things relate to each other and what needs to be done first.

The process map is a great tool to manage your team and offers credibility to lenders and potential investors. The tool is a great way to jumpstart your efforts when you are stuck. Update the map as new information becomes available.

A process plan will help you soar with condors and dance with the ants.

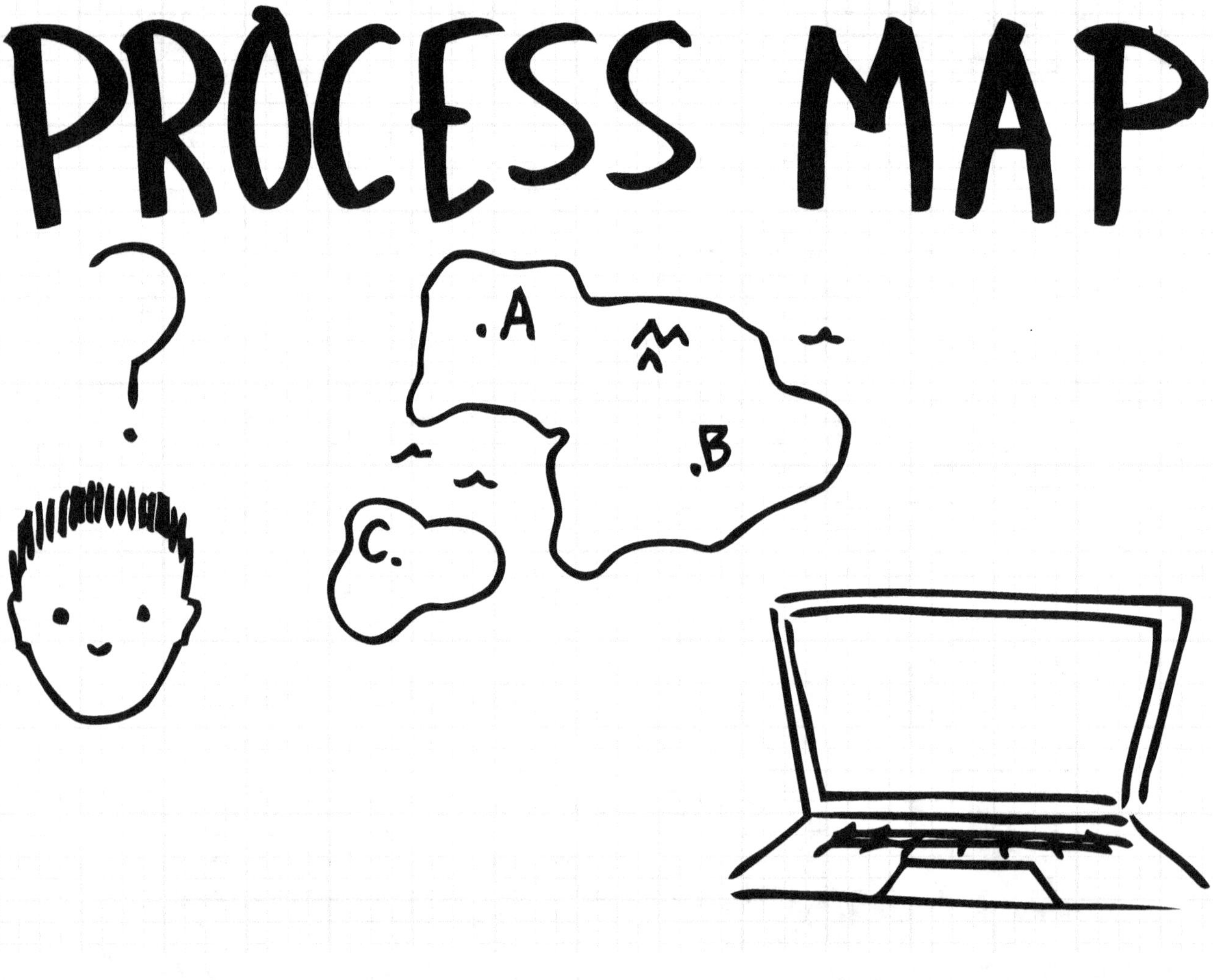

SERVICE – EXAMPLE

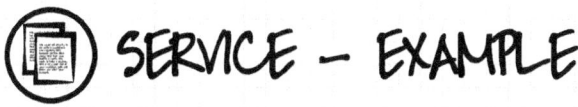

SERVICE EXAMPLE - Landscape Design			Week											
Task	Owner	Deadline	1	2	3	4	5	6	7	8	9	10	11	12
THINK														
Write out consumer experience	Mike	1/3												
Develop value chain to map out business	Mike	1/5												
Do first draft of presentation	Mike	1/7												
CREATE														
Write out key steps in landscape design process	Mike	1/10												
Show process to architects to get get feedback & revise	Mike	1/13												
Get process feedback from previous customers & revise	Mike	1/20												
Get teamfeedback & revise	Mike	1/27												
Finalize design process procedures	Mike	2/4												
TELL														
Clearly define consumer profile	Joan	1/3												
Define market position & pricing vs. competitors	Joan	1/4												
Develop message and key benefits	Joan	1/11												
Create site navigation & wireframes for website	Joan	1/23												
Write website content, get feedback and revise	Joan	1/30												
Ask around for and choose web developers	Mike	1/30												
Write brochure content	Joan	2/4												
Find and shoot pics for website & brochure	Joan	2/6												
Layout brochure	Joan	2/11												
Develop website	Joan	2/17												
Print brochures	Joan	3/2												
Find large community events where we can volunteer	Mike	3/17												
Develop flyer for distribution in target neighborhoods	Joan	3/18												
Go live	Joan	3/23												

SELL			
Map out sales cycle	Bill	1/8	
Define quality lead and track	Bill	1/13	
Develop referral incentive program for nursery workers	Bill	1/28	
Develop referral incentive program for past customers	Bill	2/4	

RUN			
Create job descriptions & interview questions	Mike	2/1	
Interview candidates for project work	Mike	3/3	
Write bio for marketing materials	Joan	3/11	
Establish legal entity?	Bill	2/9	
Apply for Employee Identification Number	Bill	2/15	
Register for sales tax	Bill	2/23	
Open bank account	Mike	2/28	
Set up bookkeeping software	Bill	2/28	
Find lawyer & tax accountant by end of year	Bill	4/3	
Track expenses	Bill	1/8	
Sales build	Bill	2/10	
Cash budget	Bill	2/23	
Do final presentation	Mike	3/17	

FAQ

1. **What if I don't know the steps?** Don't worry. As you go through the Checkup, you will learn more steps needed to complete the startup process. Look again at the question prompts in the template and examples. Another big help is to explain the processes to a friend, as these discussions often clarify what needs to be done.

Instructions

Overview: Map out the processes and steps.

1. Start with adding the major steps. Include who is responsible and set a deadline.

2. Add detailed steps. Fill in the weekly boxes to understand the time relationship between the tasks.

4. Review the entire map to ensure that the steps make sense and are timed correctly.

5. Update regularly.

CREATE

PROCESS MAP — Week

Task	Owner	Deadline	1	2	3	4	5	6	7	8	9	10	11	12

THINK

CREATE

TELL

SELL

RUN

Customer Profile
Create a customer profile.

Watch Video
www.joestartup.com/module//tell/customer-profile

My friend Deirdre asked me what a customer profile is. She is a clothing designer and novelist. A customer profile in a business is like a main character description in a novel. The profile includes the needed details to understand who the customer is. A customer profile often includes the following information:
1. Age range
2. Gender
3. Most important benefits they care about
4. How important prices are to them
5. How they research a product
6. Where they buy
7. When they buy
8. Whether they do repeat buys
9. Adjacent products they buy (e.g., toothbrush and toothpaste)
10. Which competitor product they use

A. Let's look at an example: Deidre noticed that female police officers often complained about how uncomfortable wearing bulletproof vests were. The cotton t-shirts sold in the uniform shops would get sweaty in warm weather and were not warm enough in the winter. After talking to all the female police officers she knew, Deidre wrote out a customer profile.

The profile is as follows: females aged 28–45 years who want comfortable, dark-colored undershirts in all weather conditions. They want to pay $20–$35. While many look online, they only really buy products that they can try on. The officers said they would buy twice a year—a long-sleeved shirt in the fall and a short-sleeved one in the spring.

They hope to get one year of life given that the vest constantly rubs the shirts. They would buy 10 shirts annually. Officers often buy undershirts when buying new uniforms.

Deidre made the following calculation: In the first year, the customer's annual purchase amount is 10 shirts at $30, or $300.

B. Now you can estimate how much you can spend on marketing to each customer after understanding the annual purchase amount. In Deidre's case, if the annual purchase amount is $300, $30–$50 in marketing for each customer seems reasonable. The marketing expense can range from 5% to 30% of sales.

A clear, accurate, and complete customer profile will help so much in product development and marketing. The first step is to talk to as many potential customers as possible.

Two important things to consider:

C. Customer profiles can change. In Deidre's case, male police officers started asking about the product. Have a clear profile, but be open if it changes.

D. There can be more than one customer profile in your business. In Deidre's case, she needs to sell to uniform store owners so that she can sell to the end customer, the police officers. She needs a customer profile for buyers at uniform stores.

 EXAMPLES

Margaret planned to open an upscale housewares store in a mountain resort town. Although she knew how important it was to know her customers, she just wasn't sure. She thought back to her customers at her previous job at a housewares store in NYC. Even though she had grown up in the town, she needed to carefully watch the tourist crowd to be sure things hadn't changed.

She sketched out the customer profile: 28- to 60-year-old females, mostly moms or grandmothers. They want memorable items even if they cost more. They buy memories of the trip as much as they buy housewares. Plus, they would spend more if they were on vacation; it would likely be an impulse buy. The customer wants to be surprised by seeing something really advanced, nostalgic, or colorful.

Margaret selected groups of items that could be sold together at different price points. In the end, she had a clear idea of who her ideal customer was; now, she could develop marketing materials with that target in mind.

Greg and Pete were developing a computer program using algorithms to predict where wheat prices were going. Greg was previously a state wheat agronomist who wrote reports that were closely followed by farmers and traders. Pete used to sell computer programs that traded stock to hedge funds. They weren't sure exactly who their customers were.

Greg thought they should sell monthly predictions and information to 30- to 60-year-old wheat traders and farmers across the Midwest. This group would want emailed reports monthly and the ability to communicate with Greg for $1,500–$2,000 monthly. Pete wanted to target hedge funds in New York who would invest a block of money into their wheat trading computer program. Greg and Pete wanted to eventually serve both markets, but they had to make a decision on which customer profile to use.

Ted had these great medical scrubs to sell, but he wasn't sure how to sell them. He knew that the big hospitals were not going to work since they rented scrubs from linen companies that used the cheapest scrub they could find. Ted did know that the elective surgery clinics, like plastic surgery and orthopedic surgery, wanted to look better and more professional. Plus, they had the money.

Ted had a clear idea of the customer, which would impact his marketing- and distribution-related decisions. Ted realized that his target audience was the head nurses aged 35–60 years old. They want the staff to look good and professional. As they are probably on their feet all day, they want comfort. Pricing could be an issue. Nurses likely do their research online at scrub stores and nursing conferences. They shop online once annually or at retail stores. Doctors also sign off on the purchase.

EXAMPLE - BULLETPROOF ACTIVE WEAR

	Customer 1	Customer 2
Name	Female Officers	Uniform Store Owners
Age range	28-45	35-60
Gender	Female	Male
Most important benefits they care about	Comfort in all conditions	Good margin
How important is price?	$20-35, will pay for more comfort	Very important, won't spend more than $15-18
How they research the product	Look online but want to try it on before buying	Look online and tradeshows
Where they buy	Uniform shops and then web	Sales reps and tradeshows
When they buy (impulse, long research, seasonal)	Impulse; buy with new uniforms	Oct-Nov & May-June
Is it a repeat buy? If so, what is the pattern?	Annual	Biannual with fill ins
Adjacent products? (think toothbrush & toothpaste)	Police Uniforms	Police Uniforms
Which competitor product do they use?	Cotton Tshirts, Nike, Under Armor	Sell mostly cotton tshirts
Average Units Purchased Guestimate	10	200
Average Price Guestimate	30	15
Average Purchase Amount Guestimate	300	3,000
Average Marketing Investment Guestimate	30	100
% Marketing / Purchasing (2-30%)	10%	3%

FAQ

1. **What is an average transaction amount (ATA)?** This amount is the average value that a customer buys each time from a company.

2. **What is the annual purchase amount (APA)?** This amount is the average value that a customer purchases each year.

INSTRUCTIONS

CUSTOMER PROFILE - Create by filling out below.

	Customer 1	Customer 2
Name		
Age range		
Gender		
Most important benefits they care about		
How important is price?		
How they research the product		
Where they buy		
When they buy (impulse, long research, seasonal)		
Is it a repeat buy? If so, what is the pattern?		
Adjacent products? (think toothbrush & toothpaste)		
Which competitor product do they use?		
Average Units Purchased Guestimate		
Average Price Guestimate		
Average Purchase Amount Guestimate		
Average Marketing Investment Guestimate		
% Marketing / Purchasing (2-30%)		

Positioning

Define your company's positioning.

Watch Video
www.joestartup.com/module//tell/positioning

A. Bill, an arborist, asked what positioning means and why it is important. Positioning is what your company stands for in the market compared with your competitors. With knowledge of your positioning, you can estimate the potential market size to see if there is enough need for your product.

B. Bill lists his biggest competitors from the largest to the smallest. He finds out their rates and talks to customers. He is able to map out the competitors based on best work, customer service, and price.

Bill learns that word of mouth is how most competitors get their business going. He guesses that in any given year, there are 100 homes that need service, and the average job is $5,000, given the mature trees in the area. The market value is $500,000.

C. Bill decides how he can be different. He chooses customer service where he will always return a call within an hour and will always be a little early. Bill decides not to be the cheapest but provides the best service. To jumpstart his business, he decides to create a brochure that he will leave at heavily-wooded homes after big storms.

D. Bill will leave a note with the brochure if he sees a tree that looks threatening to a nice home. Finally, he will volunteer to clear roads after storms. Bill reckons if he works hard, he can get at least 20% of the business (or $100,000) each year.

E. Determine your company's positioning given the market size and the competitors. How will you always be different from your competitors? Will you be the best product, the best customer service, or the best price?

 EXAMPLES

Rob was excited to develop a display board app, and he knew his consumer profile of interior designers, architects, and product designers. But he knew he had to get the positioning just right with this finicky crowd.

Rob researched the number of potential users who already had an iPad or tablet, which is around 1 million. He believes that every designer will be using display board apps within five years, but he estimated that convincing 20% of potential users, or 200,000, is possible. Rob researched competitor products, but there were none yet. With designer friends, he put together some mockups and tested price points of $10 with basic functionality, $20 for a medium version, and $30 with advanced functionality. Most responders suggested $10 and gave feedback about what they really needed.

Rob calculated the potential market to be $2 million for this product at the basic version. Given the designer feedback, Rob designed a simple and intuitive user interface and waited on adding bells and whistles. He decided to use "simply stylish" to reinforce the positioning. Rob was ready to go.

Courtney, a former professional dancer and her new best friend Sally, an accountant, have teamed up to create a dance studio. Once they did research, they found several dance studios in town. The existing studios were large with lots of volume. The large class sizes kept tuition down, but turnover was also high. Trying to compete on price was not attractive. Courtney's husband had signed up for golf lessons where each lesson was videotaped. The video, accessible on the web, included comments on things to work on before the next class. Her husband thought seeing the video helped his technique. Courtney and Sally researched how they could video record and provide analysis for dance. They created a chart of the local dance studios' programs and how they were marketed. The duo asked mothers of dance students about the dance studios.

Courtney and Sally estimated that there were 4,000 potential dancers in their area. However, they wanted to charge a higher price, $175 monthly or $2,100 annually, with a video analysis and Courtney's recent professional dance experience. The higher price would make the market smaller; they thought that only 15% of the overall market was relevant. The market size was estimated to be 4,000 x 15% x $2,100 or $1,260,000 million. The team decided to focus on a higher-end clientele with likely more dance experience. They settled on the tag line of "Where artistry and technology dance."

David discovered swimming later in life but always had the same problem when he swam: He would forget the number of laps he swam. During an hour, it was easy to forget one lap when you were doing 50. Other swimmers had the same problem. David wanted to do something about it—find a lap counter. He checked around and looked online. He mapped out who the competitors were and their price points. Some were big, like a clock face, that, cost little, and some were watch-size. But these were heart rate monitors and cost a lot.

He asked other swimmers what benefits they wanted: ring size, laps counted, and less than $30. They did not really want any other information. David decided to go with simple and inexpensive as the positioning and to sell through Amazon.

POSITIONING & MARKET SIZE CHART

Input information on competitors below

Competitor Name	Product	Price	Service	Size	Comment
Bill's Tree Cutting	NA	1	5	1	More expensive, more service
Christian Arborist	NA	2	4	2	Smaller, solid service and lower price
Tree Manacurists	NA	3	3	3	Middle of road service and pricing
LeVeau's Tree Cutting	NA	2	5	1	Smaller, decent service and higher price
Arborists are US	NA	5	2	5	Price leaders, iffy service
Bee's Trees	NA	4	1	4	Oldest, uneven quality and high price

Rate on scale of 1 to 5, 5 being best

Input # potential customers and their average annual purchase to get total market size.

Potenial market value		Comment
# potential customers:	100	
avg. annual purchase	$5,000	
Total market size	$500,000	
% market share	10%	The % of customers you think you can win, typically 5-50%.
Potential annual sales	$50,000	

Market size estimates potential upside and marketing spend/customer, which is 5-30% annual sales.

POSITIONING GRAPH

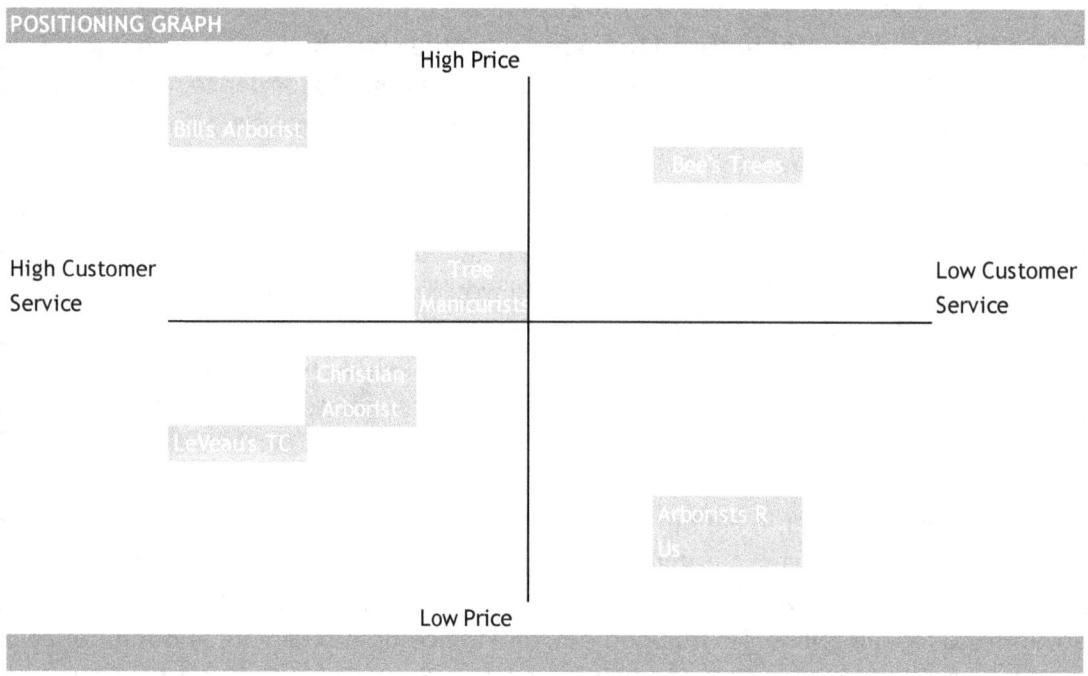

1. **What is market size?** Market size is the number of potential customers times the annual purchase amount.
2. **What are potential sales?** Potential sales refer to the market size times a percentage of the market that a company can convert into buyers.

 INSTRUCTIONS

Overview: Define your company's positioning.

1. Fill out the positioning and market size chart.

POSITIONING & MARKET SIZE CHART

Input information on competitors below

Competitor Name	Rate on scale of 1 to 5, 5 being best				Comment
	Product	Price	Service	Size	Include your company

Input # potential customers and their average annual purchase to get total market size

Potenial market value		Comment
# potential customers:		
avg. annual purchase		
Total market size		
% market share		
Potential annual sales		

Market size estimates potential upside and marketing spend/customer, which is 5-30% annual sales.

POSITIONING GRAPH

```
                    _____
                   High _
                      |
                      |
High _____         |                    Low _____
——————————————————————+——————————————————————
                      |
                      |
                      |
                    _____
                   Low _
```

Always Be Different

Decide how your business will always be different.

Watch Video
www.joestartup.com/module/tell/always-be-different

A. My friend Gigi asked me to help with her business. I asked her how her product is different from others.

Do customers care about the difference enough to choose your product? Let's talk about three companies that have differentiated themselves from others.

B. First, everyone knows about Apple's iPhone success. In the beginning, it was a breakthrough product—the idea of combining a phone, music, and different apps. Even though it has been copied, iPhone still excels because it is intuitive. It is the best product in its category.

C. Second, people are learning more about Zappos.com, a website that sells shoes at full retail price with free shipping and a one-year return policy. You can try on four to five pairs of shoes and return all but one. Their customer service is very responsive. They offer the best customer service in the category.

D. Third, everyone has felt the impact of Walmart. For every $100 of sales, they buy the product for $90, pay overhead expenses of $7, and keep the profit of $3. They have driven down costs and passed the savings onto the consumers. It is the best price in its category.

With your business, you need to decide one thing in which you want to be best. Do you have the best product, customer service, or best price? After choosing the area in which you want to be the best, you should still strive to be good at the other two areas. I think it is impossible to be the best in two or more categories. Choose wisely.

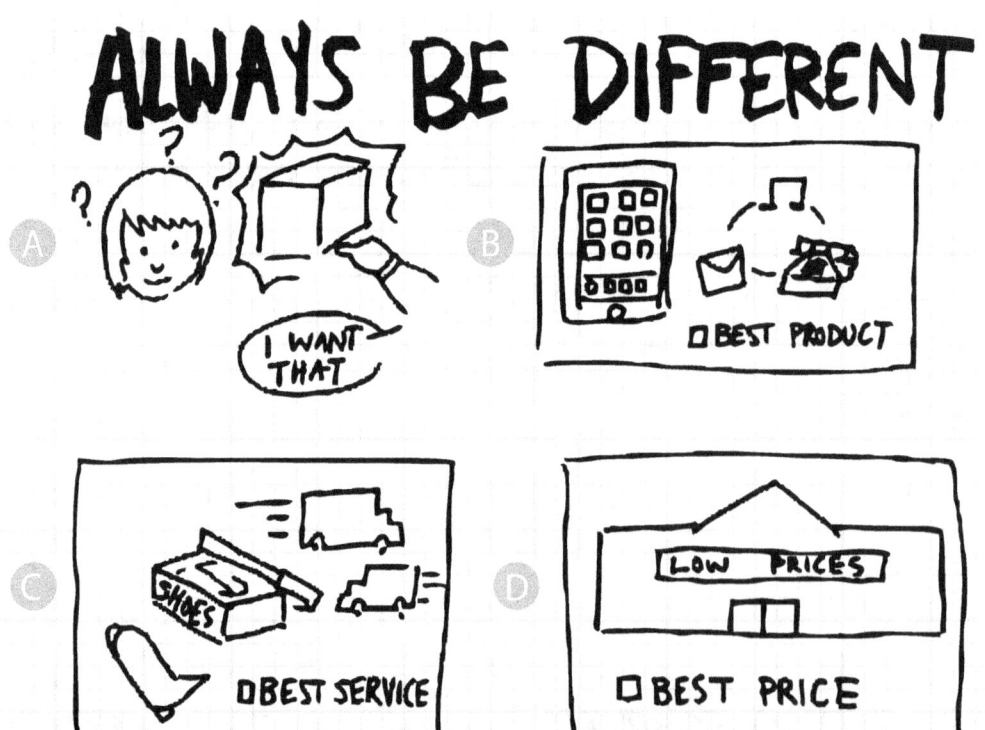

1. Here is an example: Gigi wanted to supplement her income. She noticed that her neighbors were often too busy to walk their dogs. Gigi researched the other dog-walking services. I asked her if she wanted to give the best customer service like personalized attention, shopping, and running other errands or did she want to offer the lowest cost, no frills while walking multiple dogs.

After making a decision, she could decide how to get the message and benefits across potential customers.

2. In one or two paragraphs, write out what your business will be best at: price, customer service, or product. Describe how you will achieve this goal. Describe your competitors, what they are best at, and how you will be different.

 EXAMPLES

Eli went to the farmer's market with his mother for one reason: cookies. His mother only allowed him to eat food with healthy ingredients—even cookies. The healthy cookies were $3–$4 a piece, more than his mother wanted to pay.

Eli had an idea. He would make healthy cookies in a smaller size and charge 50 cents each or a half dozen for $3. Eli knew more parents would let their kids buy smaller cookies and, likely, more of them because they seemed cheaper. Eli would offer the best price in the farmer's market and still provide a quality product.

Mario, a pizzeria owner, came in the restaurant on his off day to find a big crisis. There was an order for 30 pizzas, but the delivery boy had just quit. Mario had just come back from a Christening ceremony. He was dressed in a crisp navy suit, a white shirt, and a brilliant blue tie. He shrugged and started loading the pizzas in his car. When he showed up to the customer, the wife answered the door.

She was impressed that the pizza delivery guy was so well dressed. When she overheard Mario singing a traditional Sicilian ballad, the wife asked if Mario would sing for her husband who was celebrating his birthday. Mario declined at first, but the wife really wanted him to sing. After delivering the pizzas and opening the boxes, Mario introduced himself to the birthday man and belted out the ballad like Mario's grandfather did years ago.

The party goers were shocked and delighted, particularly the birthday man who was nearly in tears. The wife announced that everyone should buy pizza from Mario, the singing pizza delivery man. Afterward, orders from the toney seaside town flourished. While there were other pizza places, no one offered the unique customer service Mario did.

Rob develops iPhone/iPad apps. One day, he overheard his wife, Christine, an interior designer, complaining about the display boards designers use to pitch clients. The poster-size display board is a collection of photos, color choices, and fabric swatches. Christine thought the boards were clunky, and the photos of the boards that she put on her iPad could not be changed; she wanted to change photos and colors on the fly. Christine also wanted to show new clients the boards she had done for previous clients. She wanted to click through photos to get to vendor websites and add budgets.

Rob thought these iPad display boards would be really popular with young interior designers but would have a broader appeal to the creative class: architects, graphic designers, and product designers. Rob focused on creating a best-in-category product.

? FAQ

1. **What is differentiated?** Differentiated means different.

i INSTRUCTIONS

Overview: Decide how your business will always be different

Answer the following questions in one to three paragraphs.
1. What will your business do best: price, customer service, or product?

_____

2. Explain specifically how you will achieve this goal.

_____
_____
_____
_____
_____
_____

3. Describe your competitors, what they are best at, and how you will be different.

_____
_____
_____
_____
_____
_____

TELL

Message

Craft the message by highlighting the product's key benefit and developing a narrative.

Watch Video
www.joestartup.com/module/tell/message

A. My friend, Charlie, who is in the t-shirt business, asked me about how he can create a brand that is different from that of his competitors. I told him that he needed a clear message and narrative.

B. The message is the argument, or key benefit, for buying your product or service. On one page, write down all the product features and benefits. The features are the various aspects of the product. The benefits are the solutions that the features provide to the customer. Choose the most important benefits and top 2–4 features.

C. Charlie was tired of selling shirts based on price. He decided to license digital designs and print them on a digital fabric printer one shirt at a time. After preparing a list of the product benefits, he settled on the key benefit of getting a custom shirt chosen from thousands of designs. Charlie chose the brand Custom4u Tees.

After having a clear message, build a memorable story, or narrative, about the product or service. Write about how you came up with the idea. Use specific names and details, but the story should be no more than three to four paragraphs. While selling successfully is about communicating the product's benefits, people really want to hear stories.

1. Charlie used the story about how his business started. He was a struggling painter when his girlfriend left him and took all his cool T-shirts. He started making his own. Strangers asked him where they could buy the shirts. A business was born.

2. After developing a clear message and narrative, test it out on friends and family. Check if they understand the benefit quickly and if the story works for them. Be open to changes. You will likely need several revisions to get the message and narrative right.

3. Try to develop a 30 second pitch that quickly describes the product and its key benefits. In addition, develop a 2 minute pitch that includes the product, its key benefits, and a narrative about how the idea originated. This 2 minute pitch is often called the elevator pitch, or what you would tell a stranger about your business on an elevator ride. Video-tape your 30 second and 2 minute pitches. Revise them until you are satisfied.

4. Charlie told his friends his message and narrative. They loved the narrative, but Custom4u Tees did not click. At first, Charlie was not happy. He then pitched Made4u Tees. His friends liked that name much more.

5. Develop a tag line, which is a short phrase describing the key message. For example, Nike's tag line is "Just do it," which suggests action and that you are capable of achieving your goals. Charlie worked with a lot of combinations for a tagline. In the end, he chose "10,000 designs - 1 Made4u." He felt this captured his key benefit.

After you have tightened up the message and the narrative, make sure that they are used throughout all the marketing materials. Customers will then have an easier time understanding what the brand stands for. Remember that the message is your argument for why customers ought to buy your product. The narrative is the story of the product or service. The opinions of others are essential.

 # EXAMPLES

Burke loved to race mountain bikes. He often strapped a video camera to his helmet to capture the events. During one race, he flipped over his handlebars on a downhill as his bike bounced over him. Burke took his helmet off, looked with a daze, and said, "I wish I had scouted the course," before he passed out. Fortunately, Burke was not seriously injured and he posted a YouTube video called Bummer Burke. The video went viral within the mountain biking community.

A local race director asked Burke if he would video record a race course and give tips and then post the video on a race website. Burke thought a new business might be born. He could create race course videos that scouted the large mountain bike races with the actual course, GPS, and riding tips. The key benefit is that the video would help you learn the course for only $15. The narrative of the business would be the Bummer Burke video. The tag line is "Scout it out." He worked on his 2 minute pitch for meetings with race directors.

Roy developed a process to make custom jewelry where customers design the product. He just wasn't sure what the message should be. He wrote down all of the benefits and asked his target audience, moms, which features they thought were the most important. The main benefit was that their kids would be making one-of-a-kind family heirlooms. He decided that the best product narrative is the story on how he came up with the idea. His daughter had come into his studio one day and asked if she could make a piece of jewelry. Roy had given her some jeweler's wax, much like clay. When his daughter finished sculpting a pendant, she asked him if he could cast it in sterling silver so she could give it to her Nanna.

Roy told the story to moms, and they loved it. He used the key benefit and narrative in designing his website and brochures. Roy had his message.

Steve was excited to start up his Ironhorse granola business but was not sure what the message should be. He knew that the mountain bike community liked it because his friend, Conroy, a mountain bike champion, said it was his secret weapon. They liked humor and toughness. And it tasted really good. Steve mapped a survey of the granola available; there were lots of choices at all price points. Some marketed as most nutritious, cheapest, most protein, or exotic ingredients.

In the end, Steve decided to go with humor and toughness. The key benefit he decided is that it will make you "Strong like a bull," and "Tastes real good." He named his blends Intestinal "Fortitude" and "Canof Wupass", which he felt would appeal to the tough, mountain biking community.

Steve put together a 2 minute pitch on how the granola idea came up: His mountain bike champion friend pushed him to start the business because the product was so good. After selling it at several mountain bike races, Steve knew the message was perfect for his target consumer.

 **FAQ**

1. **What is a key benefit?** A key benefit is the most valued solution for the customer.
2. **What is a feature?** A feature is a characteristic of a product.
3. **What is a pitch?** A pitch is a sales argument for purchasing a product.

 **INSTRUCTIONS**

Overview: Craft the message by highlighting the key benefit and building the narrative.

1. List the product's/service's features and benefits.
___

2. Choose the key benefit and top 2–4 product features.
___

3. Write a narrative, or story, about the product. The narrative can include how the product came about or what inspired it. Selling successfully is communicating the product's benefits, but people also want to hear stories.
___

4. Test out the key benefit and the narrative with friends and family. Check if they get the message. Make changes.

5. After getting feedback from other people, make a 30 second sales pitch describing the product and its key benefit. Also, create a 2 minute pitch describing the product, its key benefit, and the narrative. Make a video, get more feedback, and make changes.
___

6. Develop a tagline—a short phrase describing the brand—which should be the key message.
___

7. Use the message and narrative consistently throughout your marketing materials. That way, customers will quickly understand what the brand stands for.

Materials

Select the best materials to reach your customer.

Watch Video

www.joestartup.com/module//tell/materials

The decision on which marketing materials to develop depends on the customer profile and budget. How does your target customer currently get product information? Is there a better, that is, clearer or more cost-effective, way? Here is a list of potential marketing materials or marketing collateral.

1. Business cards and stationery. These are great for establishing credibility. If you have the logo and tagline, then business cards are easy and inexpensive. Put key benefits on the back of the card. I like to order stationery as handwritten notes add a personal touch.

2. Brochures. These are great if you are often face-to-face with customers. While the Internet has significantly changed how marketing is done, a physical brochure still has relevance. The brochure's content is mostly done if you have completed the message and narrative. Just add photos, artwork, and testimonials.

The brochure is the physical version of the 2 minute elevator pitch. Search online for brochures you like. Draw a layout to have a clear idea of what the brochure should look like. Then, decide whether to design it yourself online or find a graphic designer to help. If you are looking for a graphic designer, get a recommendation from a friend.

3. Flyers. These work for local businesses that advertise to the public. The content usually includes the message, location, time, and catchy artwork. Look online to get flyer design ideas.

4. Catalogs. Physical catalogs are costly and go out of date quickly. Online catalogs are highly preferable if your customer can accept them. If you do have to print a physical catalog, then the message and narrative should be included, along with the product, pricing, and index. Have a look at what competitors are doing. There are so many catalogs being done badly. Consider investing in a good graphic designer to differentiate your business. Ask around for local printers, but get an online quote for comparison.

5. Website. Your web presence will likely be your most important marketing material. Invest the time to get the message, narrative, and artwork/photos right. Simple is better, particularly on the web. However, a simple and intuitive design often requires the most amount of work. I recommend a web designer if you are putting up your first website and your budget allows it. Research what your competitors and your favorite companies are doing. Emulate their best qualities. Be sure to look into search engine optimization.

6. Social media. During the next several years, Facebook and Twitter will likely become as important as your website. Develop a company Facebook page; it is easy and costs nothing. Ask family and friends to like it. Tweeting is helpful in establishing credibility for service businesses. See if there is a good return by testing Facebook ads with as little as $25–$200. Let blogs in your space know what you are doing.

7. Email. With the right customer lists, this method can be a cost-effective way to reach customers. There are many email list providers who have segmented the demographics and sell by the thousand. Realize that open rates can be 4%–20% and click-through rates can be 1%–9%. The only way to find out if this method works is to do a test.

8. Online ads. Try Google Adwords. Buy ads on competitor name searches. Make sure your company address is searchable on Google and Apple maps.

The main points are to make a business card, build a website, and create a Facebook page. Produce brochures, flyers, and catalogs only if necessary. Test email, Facebook, and online ads. You don't need to do many marketing materials, only those that will be impactful. In the end, the marketing methods you need to explore depend on the customer profile and budget.

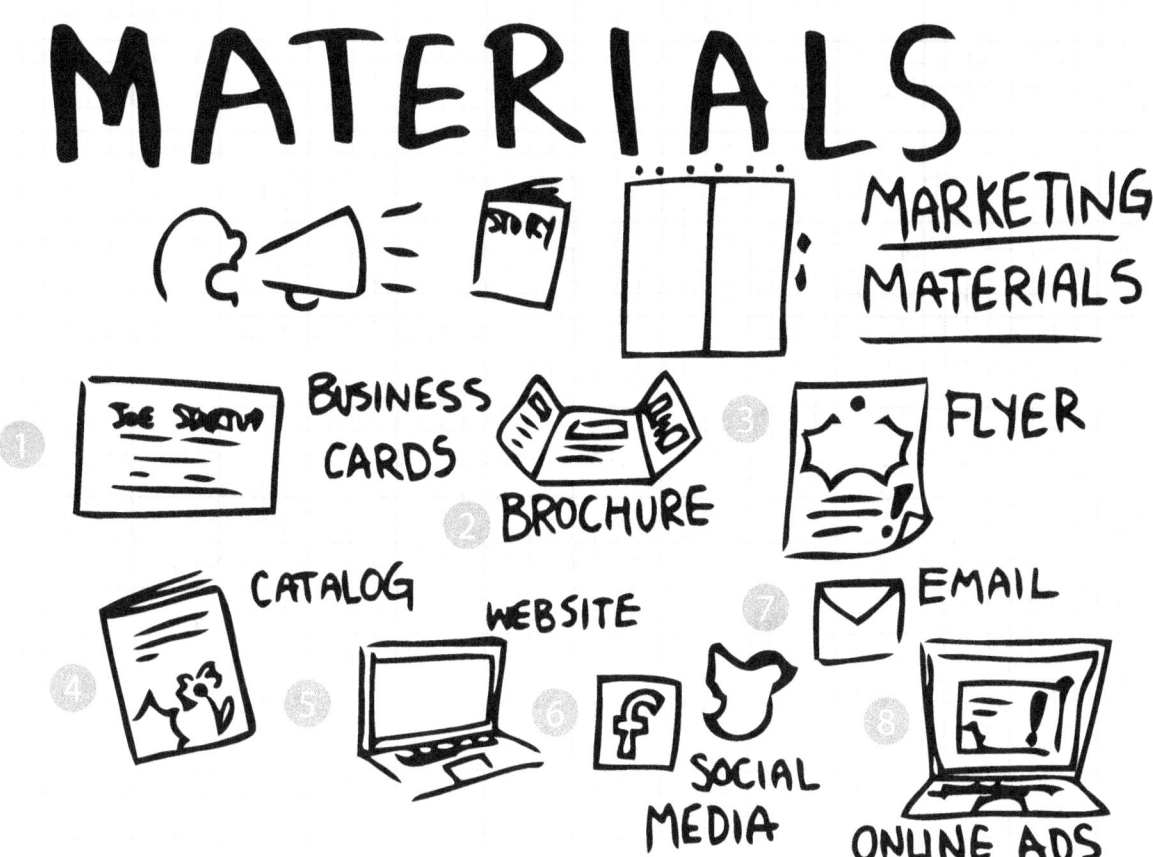

 FAQ

1. **What is a message?** A message is a clear communication to the customer that includes the product's/service's key benefit.

2. **What is a narrative?** A narrative is the story of how the product came to be or how it was inspired.

3. **What is an elevator pitch?** An elevator pitch is a 2 minute sales argument for purchasing your product. The pitch includes a product description, key benefit message, and narrative.

4. Each of these websites does a good job of walking you through the process. We receive no compensation from these companies.

Business cards and stationary:

http://www.vistaprint.com

Brochures and flyers:

http://www.mycreativeshop.com

http://www.vistaprint.com

Catalogs:

http://www.printpelican.com

Email:

http://www.verticalresponse.com http://www.icontact.com http://www.constantcontact.com

Adwords:

https://adwords.google.com/

EXAMPLES

Mike has worked at his mother's plant nursery for as long as he can remember. He didn't want to go to college because he enjoyed being outside, although he did enjoy computer games. A while back, a customer, Mr. Peters, had given Mike landscape design software to help plan out his yard. Mike really enjoyed the combination of landscape design and technology. A couple of referrals from Mr. Peters came. They all lived in the same neighborhood, which was relatively new.

Mike had worked out the narrative, pitch, and key benefits for his landscape design business. He needed to decide what materials would best reach his prospective customers. While looking through the options, he knew his customers lived primarily in three higher-end neighborhoods. Mike figured that they were web savvy, so he needed a well-done website to establish his credibility.

Mike also needed a brochure for distribution when he met with prospective customers. He created flyers since the target audience lived so close together. He could pay a kid to deliver flyers for little money. In the end, Mike went with a website, brochures, and flyers to reach his customer base.

Bill was unsure which marketing materials he should use to introduce and promote his book merchandising software venture. His target audience was independent bookstore owners, many of whom he knew. He planned to continue giving presentations at the book tradeshows. So he decided to put together a well-done brochure.

His son, Jim, was suggested an email campaign to the 1,400 independent bookstore owners. Bill thought it was impersonal and would not be effective. He wanted to do personal letters with a brochure attached. Jim thought the letter campaign was quaint but would take much work to reach a few people. Both agreed that the only way to know the best method was to experiment. They would try 20 personal letters and 200 emails. In the end, they settled on brochures, emails, and personal letters in addition to their website.

Burke was excited about his mountain bike race preview video business. But he realized he had two different consumers: race organizers and mountain bike racers. He needed marketing materials for the race organizers because he wanted to put a link on their race websites. He also needed materials for the actual bike racers themselves.

Burke prepared a brochure for race directors explaining the business, the benefits, and links to sample videos. He also developed an email to send out to race organizers with whom he would not meet face to face.

Burke expected that a video link on a race home page would generate most of his customers. He also burned DVDs with sample videos to be given away at mountain bike races. While DVDs were cumbersome, Burke thought it was worth giving a try.

MARKETING MAP - Ironhorse Granola

Customer Name	Customer Name
Endurance Athletes	Race Directors
Key Need	**Key Need**
Legal performance enhancer	Money
Message	**Message**
If you eat, then you will be "Strong Like Bull"	Your race will be cooler with unique & funny product
Key Benefits	**Key Benefits**
Nutritious	Rent
Great taste	More excitement with cool product
Great recovery	
Marketing Materials	**Marketing Materials**
Website	Email
Free samples at races	Brochure
Word of mouth	Samples

Customer Name	Customer Name
Bike Shop owners	Healthy Food Chain Buyers
Key Need	**Key Need**
Cool product	Different product and story
Message	**Message**
Yummy product that mtb celeb promotes	Differientated Product at attractive margin
Key Benefits	**Key Benefits**
Great story	Good margin
Endorsed by mtn bike celebrity	Great story
Tastes Awesome	Positioned as "real athlete" granola
Marketing Materials	**Marketing Materials**
Email	Email
Brochure	Brochure
Website	Website

Narrative

Steve loved granola and was really good at making. For years, his endurance sport buddies had said that

Artwork List	To Do List
1. Pictures of Mountain Bike Celebrity	1. Photo shoot
2. Product Photos	2. Finalize graphic designer
3. Funny cool, graphics	3. Create look-and-feel sheet

TELL

 INSTRUCTIONS

Overview: Select the best materials to reach your customer.

1. Fill out the Marketing Map below.

MARKETING MAP

Customer Name	Customer Name
Key Need	**Key Need**
Message	**Message**
Key Benefits	**Key Benefits**
Marketing Materials	**Marketing Materials**

Narrative

Artwork List	To Do List
1	1
2	2
3	3
4	4

Story

Develop bios for your team and a company executive summary.

Watch Video
www.joestartup.com/module//tell/story

A great bio and and an effective company summary may seem intimidating. They are not hard if you break them down into parts, though. A good bio is important because you will likely be using it on the website, marketing materials and any fund-raising document.

1. The first sentence should be what you would say when introducing yourself in 15 seconds. The concise description should describe your skills and experiences. In the next two to three sentences describe how you got into the startup. Convey your passion about the business. People often buy things because of the seller's enthusiasm.

2. In the next two to three sentences, describe your relevant work experiences.

Don't overdo the details, but convey that you have been there, done that. Finally, add some personal details, such as marital status, number of children, and avocations. Shared interests are a way to establish rapport with the reader. Interject a little self-deprecating humor. In the end, you would have written about yourself in 10 sentences. Once you have finished a draft, read it aloud and make any necessary changes.

3. Complete the same process for your one to three key team members by asking them to provide a bio each or by writing the bios for them. If you are going to raise money or have partnerships, you will need to write an executive summary. This exercise will force you to clearly describe your business.

1. For the company summary, describe the product and business in two to three sentences. Explain how your business is different from your competitors in two to three sentences and why the business will work in the same number of sentences.

Borrow lines from your 2 minute and 30 second product pitches.

2. Unlike the product pitches, you are selling the whole business. Finally, describe how your team is capable of executing the plan in one to two sentences. Take a look at the examples below.

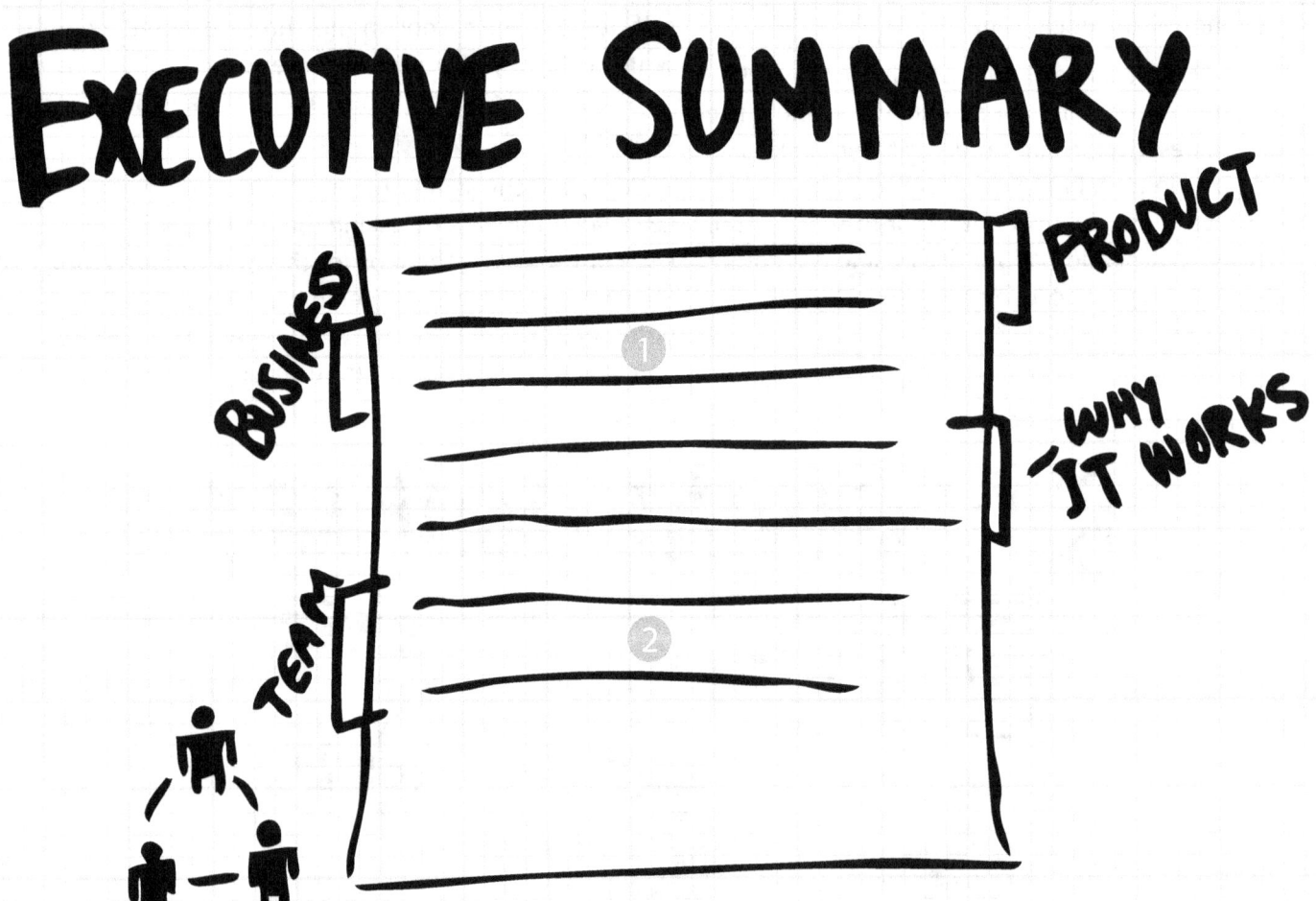

 EXAMPLES

Margaret Cell is a senior retail executive having worked in housewares for more than 11-years. She is passionate about housewares products that represent the ultimate balance between form and function. Margaret has a well-rounded career having worked as a retail associate and inventory specialist as well as being both a buyer and a merchandiser during her 11-year tenure at a premium housewares store in NYC. She studied product design at CSU and has worked part-time retail for many years. Margaret still paints watercolors and gardens when she is not chasing her 3- and 5-year-old children. She is glad to be back in her hometown where everyone knows her name.

Rocky Mountain Hardware (RMH) is a boutique housewares store located in the heart of town. The proprietor offers a well-curated selection of housewares to surprise and delight town visitors. In an aesthetically pleasing 4,500 sqf space, visitors can walk through the medley of thoughtful gifts and wow housewares while their family feasts on the yummy gelato in the back of the store. RMH offers the right product at the right time, namely, when visitors want to take a vacation and have some retail therapy. The customers are often sold by the free shipping on orders over $100 and the no-questions-asked return policy. Margaret, the owner, has worked in all aspects of premium housewares retail, holds a design degree, and is from town.

Rob Coder has been a mobile app guru for the last four years. He has an insatiable hunger for mobile apps. He completed more than a dozen native apps and has a specialty in developing highly visual intuitive content. Previously, he was a project manager at a construction company where he learned to plan out multiyear projects. He realized that a desk job suited him more than real work. Rob can design in a pinch but prefers the code. His other interests include playing riffs on his electric guitar, fly fishing, and being the best father he can be.

Designwerks develops fabulous apps for interior designers, architects, and product designers. The company's signature product, Designbord, is an iPad app through which interior designers can show clients' design boards for various projects. The product has taken off as other design professionals appreciate its intuitive interface, easy photo/artwork/video import, spreadsheet capability, and general cool factor.

While display boards and large-scale plans will always be needed, Designbord is an ultra-portable way to keep clients and team members on the same page. Plus, it enables hundreds of previous projects to be shown to prospective clients. The product is offered at an attractive, low initial price with premium pricing for additional features. Rob has been programming and developing websites and apps since the dawn of the consumer Internet.

Milo is a local agricultural sales maven focusing in honey distribution. Passionate about honey, Milo has many years of experience consuming it and making high-value-added derivatives. He has worked at farmers markets for years and harvested honey with his uncle since he was a child. He has worked in food establishments, namely, restaurants. He greatly prefers selling honey to busing tables. When not selling or consuming honey, he enjoys bass fishing and basketball.

Bee Great is one of the finest purveyors of premium honey and honey products. The company has been producing the highest-quality honey from bees who feast on the bountiful southwest Michigan wildflowers. Bee Great offers honey, bars, cookies, and toffee through farmers markets, tourist shops, restaurants, and repeat business from its website.

While competitors abound at lower prices, Bee Great has stayed with its mission of making the most awesome honey products while making sure that its story gets told to the end customer. There is a place for premium honey, especially in the go local movement. Brett has been a beekeeper, or a bee curator, since well before it has been seen as cool. He has been called a "bee whisperer." Milo has been raised in farmers markets, loves to talk sweet honey, and is an accomplished baker.

 **FAQ**

1. **What if I don't have much experience?** Emphasize the business concept, your enthusiasm for it, and how well-prepared you are for that undertaking. Identify other team members who can make up for the lack of experience on your part.

2. **What if I don't have a clear company summary?** Continue to refine the summary as you complete the Checkup. There is a successful formula to be used. Take a look at the examples and read other company summaries.

 **INSTRUCTIONS**

Overview: Develop bios for your team and an company summary.

1. Write a one-sentence summary about yourself.

2. Describe how you got into the startup and how passionate you are about the business.

3. Describe your relevant work experience.

4. Briefly describe your other interests.

5. Using the same format, complete the bios for key team members.

6. For the company summary, explain the business in two to three sentences. Look at the 30 second pitch that you wrote in the message module.

7. Describe how your business is better than the existing competitors in two to three sentences.

8. Describe the team's skills to make the business a success in one to two sentences.

RUN

Right People

Translate your business needs into finding and keeping the right people.

Watch Video
www.joestartup.com/module//run/right-people

There are three key elements needed to translate business needs into finding and keeping the right people.

1. **Translate your business needs into clear job descriptions.**

A. A finished process map is needed. Group the specific tasks that you will do on one page with your title and name. Write down general responsibilities, specific steps, tasks, and dates assigned to yourself in the process map. Do the same plan for other key positions.

Write down general responsibilities, specific steps, tasks, and dates assigned to yourself in the process map. Do the same plan for other key positions.

B. The job descriptions clearly lay out a realistic plan where everyone understands the goals. Happiness requires shared, realizable expectations. Don't assume that people will get everything by just talking about it. Your first five hires will likely make or break your business.

2. **Prepare a strong, effective interview.**

A. Good interviews require excellent preparation a clear job description and the applicants' resumes with your questions and comments. Be courteous but firm. Start out with easier questions to give the applicants a chance to warm up.

B. Ask some challenging questions to give you a clear idea of their personality and character.

Give them an opportunity to ask questions and sell themselves. Ask what their salary expectations are rather than guess. Be sure to give a brief introduction to the company.

C. Look for solid contributors. You may have to work around certain deficiencies. Superstars generally have large egos and will likely leave when the next better opportunity comes. A stable, capable team beats a short-lived superstar team.

3. Retain the best.

It is unrealistic to think that employees will stay with the company forever, but you hope that they stay through the critical period. Consider the following:

1. Meet regularly with the employee to go through the job description and, most importantly, the specific goals of the company. Be on the same page. The goal is for the employee to do the job with minimal management from you. Then you can focus on other things so the business can grow. These meetings could be as brief as 5 minutes. The key is to have structure and regular communication.

2. Create a personal development program that asks the employees to list the skills and experiences that they want to develop over the next one to three years. Ask them what their dream job is in five years. This personal development program will let the employee know that you are considering their interests as well as the company's.

3. Don't try to be the tough boss, which inexperienced managers feel they have to be. Lay out the expectations in the job descriptions and the short-term goals. Be tough when you need to be, but be gentle if the situation demands it. Don't try to be their friend, but always be courteous and friendly. Know what their personal interests are, but note that there will always be a line if you are the boss.

4. If you are working with friends or family, clear job descriptions and clearly defined goals are critical. Relationships will no doubt change. However, everything will work out if there are clear expectations and a desire to still get together for fun activities.

5. If things aren't working out after three months, make a change. Always have a three month probation period. Do yourself and your employees a favor: Sometimes things just don't work out.

EXAMPLES

Kit's honey spout business was growing but had hit a wall. He didn't have enough time to make and sell the product. Plus, he had no time to respond to beekeeping websites that wanted to sell his honey spout. Kit put the decision to hire off because he had never had anyone work for him. After talking to a family friend who worked in human resources Kit put together a job description with 1, 3, and 12 month goals. He put up a short version on Craigslist and asked for resume's and references. After getting about 15 resumes, he worked the list down to 5.

Kit set up interviews at a coffee shop. He had first-time jitters, but the job description really helped. He asked about their previous jobs and how they demonstrated hard work and responsibility and how they handled setbacks. Kit also explained the job goals. After the interviews, he worked the list down to three and called their references. He was glad he called because his first choice had a bad reference. The remaining two were evenly matched; Kit decided to go with the more outgoing one but told the other he would like to keep in touch.

Mario was nervous. He was about to interview an old friend, Peter. His friend had just closed a diner due to hard times and changing tastes. Mario, known as the singing pizza man, had many requests for a catering business. Peter was known to be set in his ways, a big concern, especially given their friendship. After talking to some friends, Mario set up an interview.

Mario started the chat with a few pleasantries as Peter was also nervous. Mario then handed a copy of a job description and emphasized the need for maximum flexibility because it was a new business. Peter remarked how formal the job seemed to be. Mario immediately interjected that they would always be friends, but now they were talking about business. They needed to have a shared view.

Mario was very honest that he worried about Peter's ability to change plans if the situation demanded. He asked Peter of instances when he did shift to changing circumstances. Peter gave a couple examples from his previous work and emphasized that he was more open to change. Mario went over the 1, 3, and 12 month objectives. Peter explained how he could meet those goals. Mario offered him the job, setting a date three months later to see if the goals were achieved. If it worked, great; if not, they could say that they gave it their best shot.

Burke's mountain bike race scouting videos were starting to generate some buzz and sales. He had hired Conrad, a superstar mountain biker, to help with creating videos and selling the videos to race directors. In awe of Conrad's riding abilities, Burke tried to be both boss and friend. Conrad was good at doing the video rides but did not really push the videos to race directors.

Burke had a couple of meetings with Conrad where he went over the job description and goals. Burke had grown frustrated that Conrad seemed not to follow up with what he promised. After each meeting, Burke sent Conrad an email stating what they discussed and the short-term goals. If Conrad was not able to fulfill the promised goals, Burke would have to let him go. Burke was at peace because he knew that he tried his best to make it work.

 **FAQ**

1. **What is a contractor?** A contractor is a person you hire temporarily to complete a specific project. A job description or contract with clear objectives is particularly important.

 **INSTRUCTIONS**

Overview: Translate business needs into finding and keeping the right people.

1. Use templates to create job descriptions and interview questions.

2. Prepare well for interviews by having clear job descriptions and specific questions about the applicant's resume.

2. Focus the questions on how the applicant's previous experiences are relevant to the job requirements and how they have overcome adversity or changes to plans.

3. Be courteous, but firm. Let them do most of the talking.

4. Meet with employees regularly to discuss specific goals and personal development plans.

RUN

Leadership

Six Steps to Lead.

Watch Video
www.joestartup.com/module//run/leadership

Let's talk about the key components of leadership. While many books have been written on this subject, I find that there are six elements which are essential.

1. Clear plan. A clear plan ensures that everyone will be on the same page. It also shows that you have thought through how all elements relates to each other. Remember that business plans and process maps change. They must be living documents that change or they will become useless.

2. Passion. Demonstrate how much you care about the business. Excitement is contagious. There will be tough times. Passion has a way of overcoming unexpected challenges.

3. Trust. The key to any long-term relationship is trust. Instill a culture of "talking the talk and walking the walk." Do what you say you are going to do, and expect the same from everyone else. That means you, too. Your employees will stay around much longer. Once achieved, delegate authority only when employees have earned your trust.

4. Step up during tough times. You will have to step up when the times get tough and things don't go as expected. Come up with a new plan and assign responsibilities. Embrace these times as they will define you as a leader. A level head in a crisis will encourage loyalty.

5. Changing your mind. It is okay to change your mind if things change. It is okay to be wrong as long as it does not cost you too much. Some new leaders believe it is a weakness to admit that they are wrong. Employees have more respect for a boss who recognizes reality for what it is, rather than trying to be right all the time. Don't be afraid to make mistakes, and learn from them instead. Just don't repeat them.

6. Empower employees to make decisions. Employees will have more ownership of a project if they are making the decisions. Once employees have gained your trust, delegate decision-making to them even if you don't agree with every decision. Intervene on the important decisions when necessary. Framing the right questions can often lead employees to your line of thinking.

While there are more traits to consider, the core principles above will take you a long way to becoming an effective leader.

 EXAMPLES

Steve's new Ironhorse Granola business was really growing with a new chef, an operations manager, and a sales representative. Then, the bottom fell out. The regional mountain bike retail chain canceled their orders because the new buyer didn't want to sell perishable food products. Steve and the team were really bummed.

Steve immediately called a company meeting to discuss their options. Steve explained how the bike chain represented 40% of sales. He was honest about how dire the situation was, but he still felt that their granola was the best. They just needed to put it in the right places to sell. Steve said that this setback is just like crashing in a mountain bike race, dusting yourself off, and getting back in the race.

After a brainstorming session, everyone agreed that each employee would try to sell the product to all retail bike stores within a 3 hour drive. The sales rep suggested that they sell the product online even if it upset current retailers. Also, the rep recommended that they sell to a local organic grocery chain. Previously, Steve had shot down both of those ideas. But reality had changed. The team agreed that they should move forward on both initiatives. Only time could tell if this plan would work, but the whole team was focused on a clear plan.

Mike ran a successful landscape design and lawn care business. But there was a bump in the road. His partner Joe was supposed to service a yard and add new bushes to a customer on a Friday. Apparently, there was a miscommunication, and the customer called absolutely livid on Friday night. She explained that they were hosting an open house for the public at 11 a.m. on Saturday.

Mike immediately contacted Joe. They avoided talking about who to blame and focused on a plan to get the work done. Mike pulled some favors with friends to get up early the next morning to service the yard from 7 to 10 a.m. When Joe and the help arrived, they saw Mike planting new bushes and flowers beyond what the customer requested. Later, Joe overheard Mike insisting to the customer that this servicing was free because of the miscommunication.

It was clear that the customer was pleased. The next week, Mike got several calls from new customers that had attended the open house and heard how great their service was.

Greg and Pete had a consulting business where their computer programs used an algorithm to forecast wheat prices. They were able to cover their expenses and pay a modest salary for themselves. The two had just started a riskier project where they would raise a fund to invest in wheat futures. The business had hired recent statistics and agronomists PhD graduates to help. After six months, there were no firm commitments for the fund.

Greg and Pete pulled the whole team together to discuss the situation. They would have to cut their salaries and lay off employees if they could not find more income. Every option would be discussed. A Chinese employee brought up how he had been asked by several Hong Kong hedge fund owners to develop a trading algorithm to trade in smaller commodity markets, such as rare earth and rubber. There were fewer sophisticated traders in these markets. Greg had nixed this idea several months ago, but he felt that they needed to consider new opportunities even though it was out of their comfort zone.

 ## FAQ

1. What if I have never led before? Don't worry; the only way to get better at leading is to lead. Have a clear plan, show passion, and follow the steps above. Be prepared to make mistakes and learn from them.

 ## INSTRUCTIONS

Overview: 6 Steps to Lead

1. Decide the most important leadership priorities to you. Write them in the text box below. Add them to your own job description.

___
___
___
___
___
___
___
___
___
___
___
___
___
___
___
___
___
___
___
___
___

SELL

Sales Cycle

Understand the sales call cycle and key performance indicators (KPIs)

Watch Video
www.joestartup.com/module//sell/sales-cycle

A. Doug, who is starting up a custom furniture company, asked how he should start selling in a big way. He should first think about the sales cycle—how a customer and a seller interact to make a sale.

B. Generating sales can seem really hard. It often is. More than likely, you will often hear "no." Rejection is no fun for anyone. But if a professional baseball player strikes out 70% of the time, he will be an all-star player. Michael Jordan missed more than half of his shots in his career; he failed in order to succeed. If you are not failing regularly, then you are not trying hard enough. The key is to have a process to create sales.

C. Let's assume that you have already put together great marketing materials. The key is to understand the sales cycle. Here are questions to consider:

1. How do you make first contact to the customer? By phone, email, or face-to-face? The latter is often the most effective and most intimidating.

2. What percentage of calls do you close? How much do customers buy on average? How many times do you need to call to close the sale? How long does it take to close?

3. What percentage of customers re-order? How many calls do you need to get a re-order? How much time is there between re-orders?

4. What percentage of customers give you leads to potential customers?

1. After being laid off, Doug decided to join his brother Wes in making custom furniture. Doug used to work with his mother, an interior designer. Doug and Wes developed a great catalog, a website, and postcards for their reclaimed wood furniture.

2. They put together a target list of customers. They guessed that they would have to see their customers three to five times before they would order. Doug asked his mother to re-introduce him to other designers. He also asked if he could set up an office in her studio at the Merchandise Mart so he would see other designers regularly.

Doug made follow-up calls to get re-orders knowing that interior designers were never sure when their next project would come.

He tried for a 25% close rate. He knew he had to stay in the mind of his customers.

3. Doug worked hard to meet other designers, realizing that the re-order business is inconsistent. He hoped that 75% of his customers would re-order within a year. Every week, Doug would try to meet with new designers and give them a catalog. He followed up with a postcard one week and one month later as a gentle reminder.

He was not shy to ask for referrals, aiming for a 66% referral rate. Doug worked hard to understand the sales cycle, realizing that what he estimated it would be might be different from what it actually was.

The sales call cycle is how the you and customer interact to make a sale. Develop a sales call model, and then refine your answers once you call on more customers.

EXAMPLES

Bill, who had a book merchandising software business, did not know what a sales cycle was. He ran an independent bookstore for many years. His son, Jim, explained that the sales cycle refers to the key steps in the sales process between a customer and a seller.

Bill reasoned that he would meet many customers at trade shows where he served as an expert speaker. He estimated that he might have to meet customers once or twice in person at the show and make three to four follow-up calls to close. Bill hoped that they could convert 50% of the customers they met at trade shows. He guessed that 80% would re-order the online service when the annual renewal was due. Bill felt that his customers would give him a large number of referrals because the independent book industry was a small yet helpful community.

Susan had started a sales award gift business, but she felt she was still missing something. She thought she could improve the sales cycle by mapping it out. She had no success trying to directly approach CEOs and Sales VPs. However, Susan could often get a meeting with the CEO's assistant or the Sales VP's assistant. She would ask the assistant for a 5 minute meeting, saying that they had to see the product to really understand it. Susan would make a custom sales award for each company that she visited.

The assistant would often get the CEO or Sales VP to take a quick look. Susan noticed that the senior managers were more available early in the mornings and late in the afternoons. She started scheduling meetings at those times. When senior managers saw the product when she visited, her close rate was 85% versus 65%. Susan found that she got prompt responses 80% of the time with an immediate personal note to the assistant and a follow-up call one week later. Re-orders happened 65% of the time within nine months. As a result, Susan sent a note to the assistants every six months. While she did not often get referrals, she was very pleased with the results. After her analysis, she really felt she had gotten the sales cycle right.

Joan's beef and bison jerky business was uneven. She wanted to grow her sales, so she mapped out the sales process. Sales in the meat shop in Montana were not hard as tourists wanted to buy authentic Montana jerky. The re-order rate was only 25%, which seemed low given how much customers said they loved the taste.

Joan wanted to contact the customers one month after they purchased. However, she felt that telephone calls were too invasive and emails were impersonal. She experimented with sending postcards with Montana landscapes with a handwritten "Howdy" and a sentence about the weather or news. Her re-order rates more than doubled when she used the postcards. Once a re-order came in, she would make sure that the customer would get a postcard every two months. Her referral rate was low, but the re-order growth made her sales cycle mapping worthwhile.

EXAMPLE - PRODUCT

Example: Doug and Wes Custom Furniture Business
SALES CYCLE

Contact

referrals, mom intros & word of mouth
postcards & catalogs
industry events
7 customer visits, 4 days a week

Close

25% close rate
avg $15,000
3-5 visits
6 month time frame
"chance meetings"

Re-order

75% re-order
avg $15,000
2-3 visits
up to 1 year
update catalog

Referral

66% referral
follow up postcards
update catalog

Key Performance Indicators - KPI

Time	Month 3	Month 6	Month 12
# Daily visits	7	7	7
% Close	15%	20%	25%
Avg. Transaction Amount	$15,000	$15,000	$15,000
% Reorder	75%	75%	75%
% Referral	50%	66%	75%

EXAMPLE - SERVICE

Example: Bill's Book Merchandising
SALES CYCLE

Contact
Referrals & word of mouth
Website
Brochure
Tradeshow speaking engagements
15 visits/tradeshow

Close
50% close rate
avg $750 monthly
3-5 visits
6 month time frame
face-to-face close often

Re-order
90% re-order
avg $500
industry show meetings
up to 1 year
update version

Referral
50% referral
follow up postcards

Key Performance Indicators - KPI

Time	Month 3	Month 6	Month 12
# Daily visits	15	15	15
% Close	20%	30%	50%
Avg. Transaction Amount	$750	$750	$750
% Reorder	90%	90%	90%
% Referral	50%	50%	50%

 **FAQ**

1. **What are key performance indicators (KPIs)?** KPIs are the driving activities and measures in your business. These often include factors that affect sales, such as the number of sales visits, conversion rates, and average transaction amounts. They include key profits and costs like raw materials prices. Each business has specific drivers. Identify KPIs and set realistic targets in appropriate time frames, such as three months, six months, and one year. Change targets once real data are obtained. Build a plan to achieve targets. This plan should be central to the company's activities.

 **INSTRUCTIONS**

Overview: Understand the sales call cycle and KPIs.

1. The sales cycle entails breaking down the sales process into stages. Answer questions in the chart below.

2. Determine what the KPIs are, namely, the key activities and measures that drive your company's growth or profit. Create realistic targets.

SALES CYCLE

Contact

Close

Re-order

Referral

Key Performance Indicators - KPI

Time	Month _	Month _	Month _

SELL

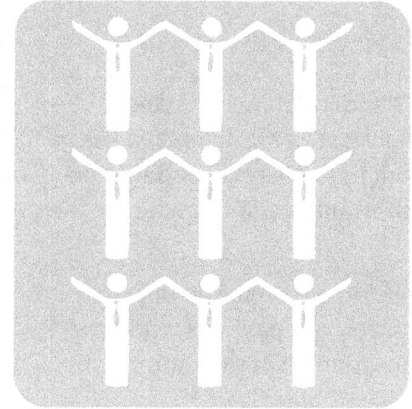

Sales Force
Decide what sales force is the best

Watch Video
www.joestartup.com/module//sell/sales-force

Doug, a furniture maker, asked how to build a sales force. He has been doing sales by himself and knows that he could get more business if he had help.

In the beginning, you will likely be directly selling to customers. During the first 6–12 months, direct selling is a great way to confirm the sales cycle and metrics. The immediate feedback is invaluable. After you have sorted out the sales cycle and sales metrics, you can decide what type of sales force is needed.

This decision requires balancing what the customer wants, the company generating enough sales, and the sales rep earning enough income. There are at least four ways to go.

1. Direct sales. This method is attractive in that you or your employees will always be in direct contact with the customer. The trade off is between direct customer contact versus higher cost. The key decision is whether a sales rep can create enough sales and profit to justify their cost. A sales rep typically gets a base salary plus a sales commission. Check what other competitor companies pay to get an idea as to what the compensation should be.

2. Independent sales reps. These reps will sell a range of products from different companies to certain customers in the same territory. For example, an independent sales rep calls on furniture stores and interior designers. The rep could sell sofas from one company, lamps from another company, and fabric from yet another company. This method entails paying a 5%–20% commission with no salary to sales reps.

This method helps companies reach many customers while not having fixed expenses. The downside is having no direct contact with the customer. The best way to recruit independent reps is to ask your key customers who their favorite reps are.

3. Distributors. These reps are similar to independent sales reps but will often buy inventory from you. However, they expect a 20%–40% commission and pay for the product 60–90 days after it is received.

4. Call centers. In call centers, employees or outsourced representatives contact potential customers by telephone. This method is often best when you have a large number of potential customers but low conversion rates. Reps are trained to use scripts and frequently asked questions. The reps are usually paid a low hourly wage with a small commission.

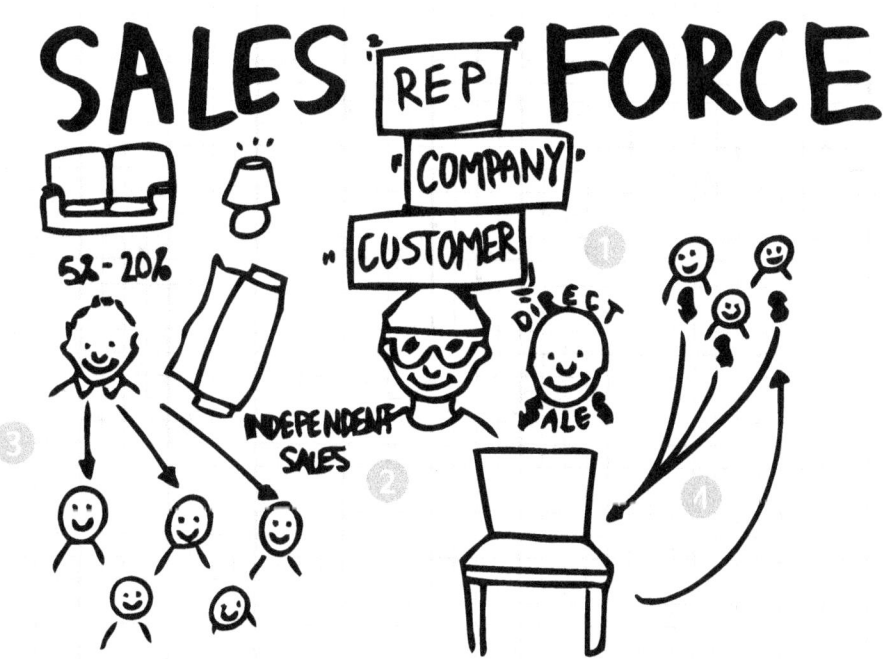

1. My friend Doug, the furniture maker, was in a quandary after a year in business. He needed help to cover all the designers in the area. His current sales were not enough to hire a full-time rep and pay himself, so he would have to hope that the rep immediately covered his salary. He was thinking about hiring his niece for the summer and paying her $12/hour to call designers in Milwaukee.

2. Doug was also considering hiring an independent rep for Chicago's North Shore, a place he had no time to visit.

Finally, Saul, an old family friend in Anaheim, asked if he could be a distributor on the West Coast. In reality, Doug wasn't sure what would work best. He reckoned that he would try each option for six months and then decide the best direction to take.

3. Think about the best sales force type based on your customer profile, how much you can pay reps, and how much reps need for compensation. Experiment until you find the right combination.

 EXAMPLES

Tim was a sales rep at an office supplies company that had recently gone out of business. The company could not compete with the big office product retailer pricing. Tim had 50 loyal customers because he always took care of things quickly and none of his customers wanted to manage their own office supplies. If they needed something, then Tim would get it for them. After doing some research, he realized that he could buy office supplies from the big box retailers, mark it up, and sell for the similar pricing of his old company.

Tim found that smaller companies would rather pay a small premium if someone outside the organization would manage their office supplies. He had the processes in place to grow the business, but he was the only one sales representative. He needed more sales help but did not want to hire an employee. Tim considered other options.

A distributor, who took inventory and resold made no sense because there would be no profit. A call center would not work because the business was built on referrals. An independent sales rep did not quite fit. Tim reconsidered hiring a sales rep. He would hire two to three young, aggressive reps by paying a salary and commission with a three-month probation period. Tim made sure that the economics worked for him and the rep.

Susan's gift business was growing, but she was the limiter. She was the only sales rep. A call center approach would not work because her business required face-to-face selling. She could not rely on independent reps as they sell many products. Susan could not afford full-time reps in the beginning. Several weeks later, she was on an online parenting forum for moms who were previously sales professionals.

Susan contacted one of the members, Donna, with the idea that the latter would call on accounts part time on a commission basis. Donna's profile was that of previously being a very successful pharmaceutical rep who missed selling but didn't want to work full time. Donna was interested in trying. Susan talked through the economics and they decided to go forward.

Alex's running apparel sold well through a large running retailer. He knew that he had to get his product placed with other retailers. Alex could not afford to hire full-time sales reps. A call center would not work with busy retailers. He contacted several sales reps of smaller running shoe companies to gauge their interest in selling his apparel on commission. He knew that times were tough, and reps could use extra money. Alex found three who would give it a try.

FAQ

1. **What is a sales cycle?** The sales cycle entails breaking down the sales process into stages.

2. **What is a sales force?** The sales force is the type of sales people who sell your product. These include direct sales employees, independent sales reps, distributors, and call center reps.

3. **What is direct sales?** Direct sales involve company employees selling directly to the end customer.

4. **What are independent sales reps?** Independent sales reps are people who are not employees of the company but sell your product and receive a sales commission.

5. **What are distributors?** Distributors are other companies who sell your product by taking inventory and receiving a commission when the product is sold.

6. **What is a call center?** A call center is a group of people who call out to potential customers. The call center reps usually receive a low base salary and a sales commission. This center can be in the company or outsourced to another company.

7. **What are sales metrics?** These are measurements that drive sales growth. Actual results should be compared to targets, or objectives, to determine sales success. Sales metrics are often included in KPIs.

8. **What is a trade off?** A trade off involves making a decision between two choices, and weighing the advantages and disadvantages.

9. **What is a base salary?** A base salary is a set amount of money that is given to a sales rep.

10. **What is a sales commission?** A sales commission is usually a certain percentage, 1%–15%, of the amount of product sold, usually over a month.

11. **What is sales compensation?** Sales compensation is base salary plus sales commission.

12. **What are sales conversion rates?** Sales conversion rates are the percentage of the total customers that are convinced to buy a product.

13. **What is outsourcing?** Outsourcing is having a business activity done by an outside company, such as a call center or sales.

INSTRUCTIONS

Overview: Decide what sales force is the best.

1. Write out the pros and cons of the different sales force types: direct, independent, distributor, and call center.

_____
_____
_____
_____
_____

Cash Budget

Forecast a budget.

Watch Video
www.joestartup.com/module//run/budget

A. My friend Alex, the running apparel guy, asked me how to do a cash forecast. He has products and orders but is not sure if he has more money coming in than going out. Cash budgets can seem so daunting. But, a simple cash budget is so empowering as owners have a clear picture of reality.

B. The process is not as complicated when you break it down into parts. Like a puzzle, fit one part at a time. Remember that reality rarely happens the way you forecast. Forecasts are made to be changed based on the best information available. Watch the video for more detail.

EXAMPLES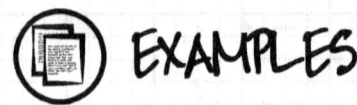

Eli's Cookies

SALES BUILD												
Month	1	2	3	4	5	6	7	8	9	10	11	12
# Products Sold	200	200	225	225	225	250	250	250	300	300	300	300
Avg. Sales Price	3	3	3	3	3	3	3	3	3	3	3	3
Total Sales (Units X Price)	600	600	675	675	675	750	750	750	900	900	900	900
Product Costs	250	250	265	265	265	290	290	290	290	290	290	290
Marketing Expenses	90	90	100	100	100	110	110	110	110	110	110	110
People Expenses	80	80	90	90	90	100	100	100	100	100	100	100
Other Expenses	50	50	50	50	50	70	70	70	70	70	70	70
Total Costs	470	470	505	505	505	570	570	570	570	570	570	570
Cash Flow	130	130	170	170	170	180	180	180	330	330	330	330
Total Cash		260	430	600	770	950	1,130	1,310	1,640	1,970	2,300	2,630

FAQ

1. I don't know where to start? Don't worry. Start with the base forecast and complete the sales forecast, and then add in the expenses. Look at the examples. Meet with a friend who knows how to do budgets. The only way to get better with handling budgets is to do them over and over.

 INSTRUCTIONS

Overview: Forecast a budget.

1. Input the estimated number of products sold, the average sales price and expenses. Calculate the cash flow, or revenue less sales. Aggregate the cash needed for total costs.

2. Watch the online video and review the online templates for more detail.

3. Budgets are complicated, but break them down into pieces. Remember that a budget helps you figure out if you have more money coming in than going out. Keep a cash forecast simple as you will likely update and use it more.

FORECAST

Month	1	2	3	4	5	6	7	8	9	10	11	12
# Products Sold												
Avg. Sales Price												
Total Sales (# Units X Price)												
Create - Product Costs												
Tell - Marketing Expenses												
Run - People Expenses												
Other Expenses												
Total Costs												
Cash Flow (Sales less Costs)												
Total Cash (Last mth plus This mth)												

SELL

Fund Raising
Understand the fund raising process

Watch Video
www.joestartup.com/module//sell/fund-raising

Fund raising is never easy. The key is to raise enough money for the project assuming that there will be setbacks. Do a well-thought-out cash forecast to determine how much capital is required. Raise 20% more money than you think you need. Ideally, you raise money from someone you trust.

Here are four common ways to raise money:

1. Ideally, you presell your product or service. Try to get paid before you make the product.

2. Ask suppliers if you can pay after you get paid by your customers. While they may not be able to do it all, they could help some.

3. Borrow money for a certain amount of time, and pay an interest rate. The loan is typically from a family member or a friend. Use banks financing if its available. Be sure that the borrower is aware of the risks.

4. Sell shares in your company in exchange for cash. For example, say your company has 100 shares and you sell 10 shares for $10. In the end, they own ~10% of the company and you have $10. If you choose to raise equity, then ask friends or advisers about what percent of the company you need to sell and for how much. There is no single right answer, but there are generally accepted ranges depending on the risk and reward.

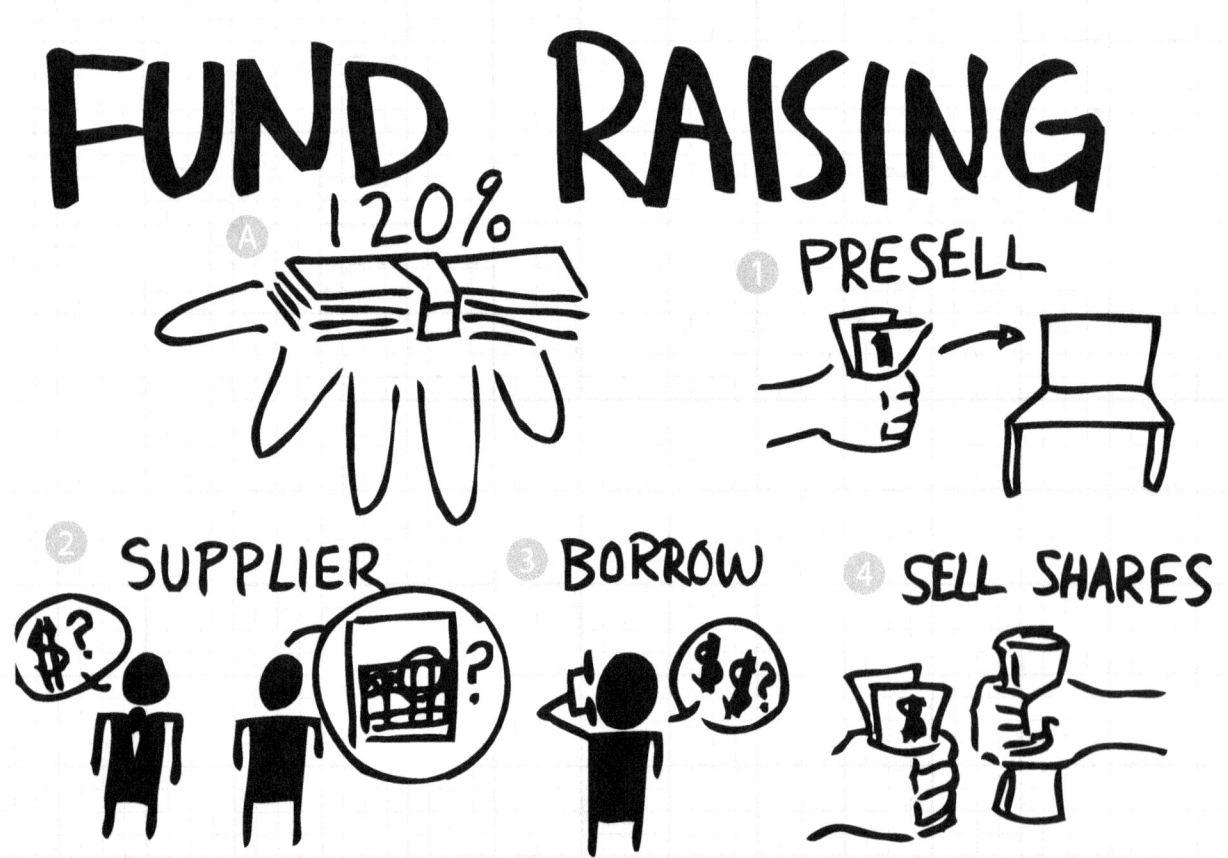

Here are the most common steps in fund raising:

1. Prepare documents, including an executive summary, a business plan, a presentation, a project plan, and a forecast. The Joe Startup plan helps with all of these documents.

2. Develop a potential investor/lender list. Approach people you know who can afford to invest. Ask friends for suggestions.

3. Send out an email with a simple introduction of one or two paragraphs. Attach an executive summary and a bio. Suggest specific times for follow-up meetings or phone calls so you can get faster feedback.

4. If they request more information and you have intellectual property you want to protect, ask them to sign a nondisclosure agreement (NDA). This short document is an agreement where both parties agree not to talk about the business to outsiders.

5. Once they sign the NDA, send the documents to them. In Joe Startup, you send them the link to the Startup plan page. Suggest specific follow-up meeting or phone call times for faster feedback.

6. If the investor is interested, either you or the investor will prepare a term sheet that describes the deal. If you want to have greater control, prepare the term sheet yourself. At this point, look for a lawyer to help with the term sheet and other documents, including a share purchase agreement and shareholders' agreement.

7. Once the agreements are signed and exchanged, the investor will send you a check or wire transfer. Celebrate briefly, but realize that this is when the real work begins.

8. Negotiating term sheets and documents is an emotional roller coaster. It is not over until the money is in your account. Deals often fall apart, so don't count on anything until it is done. Remember that the investor is trying to get the best deal possible for themselves, often at your expense. Be realistic.

 # EXAMPLES

Rob's display board app for interior designers and architects was doing well. Based on feedback, he had some clear ideas for a visually stunning version 2 but would cost $300,000 to build. While he could wait for sales for the version 1 display board app to happen, he worried that competitors would copy his idea.

Rob knew the drill of putting the investment docs in place: presentation, business plan, project plan, and forecast. He wanted to be seen as a business person, not just a hacker. He sent out initial emails to venture capitalists, but they wanted more than 50% of the business.

Rob decided to use his network of high-net-worth individuals who were in the design world. He could find three or four investors to put in $75,000–$100,000 and to help in other ways. He had initial meetings with each of the 10 potential investors and demo-ed the version 2 display board app. Afterward, he sent a NDA and other investment documents to those still interested. With the holidays coming, he wanted to get the deal done. Fortunately, he had enough investors interested to push the project forward.

Alex needed more money to buy inventory for his apparel business. He sold to a large running retailer where the product would sit for months and then sell out in one month. Alex prepared all the documents: presentation, business plan, forecast, and project plan. He met with the president of the large running retailer to discuss prepaying, or making a deposit, for the product for six months. However, the president declined, saying that they were having cash flow issues, too.

Alex met with his fabric and printer supplier, but they passed as money was tight. While Alex was discouraged, his running buddy said he should see if other runners in the community would help. Alex organized a weekend fun trail run for 30 potential investors. He gave each participant a running shirt customized for this event. He made a brief pitch and handed out materials to interested parties. He guaranteed that all investors would get a lifetime supply of running apparel if they became investors. He would follow up in the coming weeks. Time will tell.

Courtney wanted to start a dance studio but did not have the money. She had a presentation, a business plan, a forecast, and a project plan. She asked friends what ideas they had for potential investors because she knew the bank couldn't help. After getting feedback, here were the potential options: get 20 families to prepay for three years, ask the landlord to give a 50% subsidized rent for the first year (his wife was a patron of the arts), and ask her partner, Sally, to invest $30,000 for another 10% ownership in the business.

Courtney sent out emails to related parties. She organized three events for 30 families at her home studio. After a lesson, she handed out the presell document. If parents would prepay for three years, their children would not have to pay any more dues until they turned 18.

Courtney then arranged a meeting with the potential landlord after sending him the investment documents. In the meeting, Courtney would push for how good the studio would be for the local arts community. If that would not work, she would be prepared to give up 10% ownership of the studio.

Finally, Courtney set up a meeting with her partner Sally about investing $30,000 more for another 10% ownership in the business. Sally had prepared the documents and knew the challenges they faced. Courtney knew it would be hard work to raise money; she was well prepared.

FUND RAISING

Task	Owner	Deadline	Week 1	2	3	4	5	6	7	8	9	10	11	12
RUN														
Prepare documents														
-Business plan														
-Forecast														
-Project plan														
-Presentation														
Develop investor list														
Create email content														
Send out email														
Receive feedback														
Prepare NDA														
Get NDA signed														
Send out documents														
Meet face-to-face														
Prepare materials														
Prepare term sheet														
Negotiate terms														
Sign agreements														
Receive wire transfer														

 **FAQ**

1. **What is a nondisclosure agreement (NDA)?** A nondisclosure agreement (NDA), also known as a confidentiality agreement (CA), is a legal agreement between two parties that outlines confidential material that the parties want to share with one another but want to restrict access by other parties.

2. **What is a term sheet?** A term sheet is a nonbinding document outlining the terms and conditions of a business agreement between two parties. This document is usually a precursor to formal legal agreements.

SELL

(i) INSTRUCTIONS

Overview: Understand the fund-raising process.

1. Fill in the information on the task owner, proposed dates, and the weekly process map below.

2. The process is an emotional roller coaster. It's not done until it's done.

FUND RAISING

Task	Owner	Deadline	Week 1	2	3	4	5	6	7	8	9	10	11	12
RUN														
Prepare documents														
-Business plan	Joe	1/13	■	■										
-Forecast	Jim	1/21		■	■									
-Project plan	Jim	1/21			■									
-Presentation	Joe	1/21			■									
Develop investor list	Jim	1/14		■										
Create email content	Joe	1/25				■								
Send out email	Jim	2/1					■							
Receive feedback	Joe	2/8						■						
Prepare NDA	Jim	2/2					■							
Get NDA signed	Jim	2/14							■					
Send out documents	Jim	2/21								■				
Meet face-to-face	Jim	3/1								■				
Prepare materials		3/8									■			
Prepare term sheet		3/15										■		
Negotiate terms		4/6												■
Sign agreements		4/24												
Receive wire transfer		4/30												

SELL

FINAL THOUGHTS

You are ready to fix your business gaps if you have completed this workbook. Have a clear, updated plan so your don't waste your time and money. Business, like life, is about making clear tradeoffs. Change course when reality dictates. Be absolutely relentless but take breaks in the marathon called "small business." Find the right team to complement you. Always be sure there is a really good chance that the economics – more money coming in than going out – work.

Entrepreneurship is about being nimble, which requires creativity, collaboration and critical thinking. It's mostly about being creative – doing or expressing something uniquely and profitably different than others.

There is so much advice about small business. I have distilled my favorite tips:

Talk to 30 customers before you start anything.
Get advice from mentors. Test your prototype with customers whom you don't know.
Business is about making a guess, doing research, trying it, and changing the guess until it reflects reality. The only way to do a startup is to repeat over and over until it is correct.
The hand of the market will tell you what it wants, if you ask enough times.
There is no such thing as failure, only feedback.
Don't be afraid to be wrong often; try to have the mistakes not cost too much.
Plan the work; work the plan; quickly change the plan when reality tells you to.
Spend equal time on your weakest areas until they are no longer weak.
Ideas are important, but execution is much more important.
Getting knocked off is such a small probability compared to the boost of getting as much help as you can.
Perfection is the enemy of entrepreneurship. Just try it.
Don't raise funds until you absolutely have to.
You are living the dream if you wake up and you pursue your passion, purpose, and profit. Live the dream.
If the business is in a rut, try something different. Now.
To eliminate gaps, hire a capable person, short term. Let the wrong people go ASAP.

For more insights, follow the blog at www.JoeStartup.com/blog. Join our community. Join the revolution. Grow simply. Simply grow.

www.ingramcontent.com/pod-product-compliance
Lightning Source LLC
Chambersburg PA
CBHW081136170526
45165CB00008B/2697